Unseen Poetry
Exam Board: AQA

It can be tricky to analyse unseen poems in the AQA GCSE English exam, that's why we made a second book to give you even more practice, as a treat.

And that's why this CGP book is so darn good. It's packed with sample poems, worked examples, exam-style questions, expert advice and much more... everything you'll need to write a top-grade answer.

We've even included answers at the back, so it's easy to check your work. It's the best Unseen Poetry exam prep by miles — no hyperbole!

GCSE English
The Poetry Guide

Book Two

Published by CGP

Editors:
Claire Boulter
Siân Butler
Eleanor Claringbold
Alex Fairer
James Summersgill
Matt Topping
Sean Walsh

With thanks to Rachel Craig-McFeely for the proofreading.
With thanks to Emily Smith for the copyright research.

ISBN: 978 1 78294 926 8
Printed by Elanders Ltd, Newcastle upon Tyne.
Clipart from Corel®

Based on the classic CGP style created by Richard Parsons.

Contents

What You Have to do in the Exam

You'll be sitting two exams for your **AQA English Literature** course. This book will help you to prepare for the **Unseen Poetry** section in **Paper 2**, which will test you on two poems that you **won't have seen** before.

This is how your Paper 2 exam will work

1) The Paper 2 exam lasts for **2 hours and 15 minutes**. It will be split into **three sections** like this:

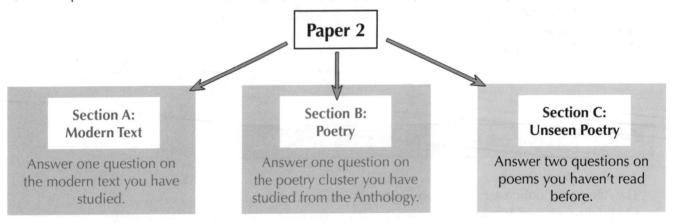

Paper 2

Section A: Modern Text

Answer one question on the modern text you have studied.

Section B: Poetry

Answer one question on the poetry cluster you have studied from the Anthology.

Section C: Unseen Poetry

Answer two questions on poems you haven't read before.

2) For **Section C** you will be given **two poems** that you haven't read before and will have to answer **two questions** about them.

3) In the exam, you should spend about **45 minutes** answering the questions in **Section C**.

You will have to answer two questions about the unseen poems

1) **Question 1** is worth **24 marks** and will ask you to analyse **one poem**. Your answer should cover:

   - **What** the poem is **about** — the poem's **message**, **themes** and **ideas**.
   - **How** the poet uses **form**, **structure** and **language** to **communicate** these ideas.

2) For **Question 2** you'll have to **compare both poems**. This question is worth **8 marks**.

3) You should write about **similarities** and **differences** between the two poems. Your answer to this question must focus on the **techniques** the poets use, such as **form**, **structure** and **language**.

4) Question 1 is worth **a lot more marks** than Question 2, so in the exam make sure you spend **more time** on your answer to **Question 1**.

The examiner is looking for four main things

To **impress the examiner** with your answers to the questions in Section C, you need to:

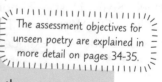
The assessment objectives for unseen poetry are explained in more detail on pages 34-35.

1) Show that you **understand** what the poems are **about**.
2) Write about the **techniques** used in the poems.
3) **Support** every point you make with **quotes** or **examples** from the poems.
4) Use the **correct technical terms** to describe the techniques used in the poems.

Five Steps to Analysing the Unseen Poems

The next three pages talk you through what to do when you come across a poem you **haven't seen before**. Screaming and running away **don't** feature anywhere — just rock-solid advice on **analysing** the poem.

Follow these five steps to analyse unseen poems

There are **five main steps** that you need to follow to **analyse** and **write about** a poem you've never seen:

1) Work out **what the poem's about** — you need to identify its **subject** and **voice**.

2) Identify the **purpose**, **theme** or **message** — work out the **overall message** of the poem before you start to analyse it in more depth.

3) Explore the **emotions**, **moods** or **feelings** in the poem — e.g. is the poem positive or gloomy?

4) **Identify** the **techniques** used in the poem — think about the **language**, **form** and **structure**. Think about **how** the poet uses these techniques to **create meaning** and **affect** the **reader**.

5) Give a **personal response** — make sure to include **your thoughts** and **feelings** about the poem.

Don't try to look for **all** of the features the **first time** you read through the poem.

Instead, **read** the poem over a **few times**, working through each of the steps **in turn** — this will help you get a **clearer understanding** of the poem and keep your analysis **focused** and **relevant** when you start writing.

1) Work out what the poem's about

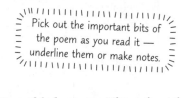

Pick out the important bits of the poem as you read it — underline them or make notes.

1) Work out the **subject** of the poem.
E.g. "The poem is about the narrator's relationship with his parents".

2) Look at whether it's written in the **first** person ("I"), **second** person ("you") or **third** person ("he / she / they").

3) The poem's **voice** can have a big **effect** on how its subject is conveyed — e.g. a **first-person** voice can make the poem sound **personal**, as if the narrator is expressing their **private thoughts**.

4) Think about **who** the poem is **addressing**, e.g. the narrator's lover or the reader.

2) Identify the purpose, theme or message

1) Think about **what** the poet is saying, **why** they've written the poem, or what **ideas** they're using.

2) The poem could be an **emotional response** to something. It might aim to **get a response** from the **reader**, or put across a message or an opinion about something.

3) There could be **more than one** purpose, theme or message in the poem — e.g. a poem might be written to **entertain**, but also to **inform** the reader about an important issue.

3) Explore the emotions, moods or feelings

1) Think about the **different emotions or feelings** in the poem.

2) Identify the poem's **mood** or **atmosphere** — think about **how** the poet has created a certain atmosphere in the poem with language, structure and form (see step 4).

3) Look out for any sudden **changes** in the mood — they could **highlight** an **important idea** in the poem.

4) Make sure that anything you say about mood and emotions is **relevant** to your argument.

5) Don't forget to **explain** the **effect** of the poem's mood on the reader.

Five Steps to Analysing the Unseen Poems

4) Pick out the techniques used in the poem

1) Think about the **different techniques** the poet has used to create the **emotions**, **moods** or **feelings** in the poem. Make sure you use the correct **technical terms** when you write about these techniques.

2) Comment on **why** the poet has used these techniques, and what **effect** they create.

3) **Don't** just **list** the poetic techniques used — choose examples that are **relevant** to your argument.

Identify the poem's form and structure

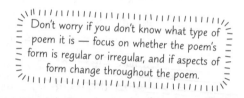
Don't worry if you don't know what type of poem it is — focus on whether the poem's form is regular or irregular, and if aspects of form change throughout the poem.

1) **Form** refers to features such as the **type of poem**, the number and length of **lines** and **stanzas**, **rhyme scheme** and **rhythm**.

2) Here are some **common elements** of form to look out for:

Type	Features
Blank verse	• iambic pentameter • no rhyme scheme
Dramatic monologue	• first-person narrator • addresses an implied audience
Free verse	• no rhyme scheme • irregular rhythm and line lengths
Sonnet	• 14 lines • regular rhyme scheme • often uses iambic pentameter • usually used for love poetry

Rhyme	Features
Alternating (ABAB)	• 1st and 3rd lines rhyme • 2nd and 4th lines rhyme
Half-rhymes	• Words that have a similar, but not identical, end sound, e.g. "<u>bread</u>" and "<u>shade</u>"
Internal rhyme	• Two or more words rhyme, but at least one of them isn't at the end of the line, e.g. "On all at <u>stake</u>, can <u>undertake</u>"
Rhyming couplet	• A pair of rhyming lines that are next to each other

Rhythm	Features
Iambic pentameter	• 10 syllables per line, alternating between an unstressed and a stressed syllable
Iambic tetrameter	• 8 syllables per line, alternating between an unstressed and a stressed syllable

3) **Don't** just **identify** the poem's form — think about **why** a particular aspect of form has been used. Consider the **effect** it creates and how it helps to convey the poem's **central ideas**.

4) **Structure** is about **how ideas progress** through the poem and any **changes** in mood or **tone**. Look at how the poem **begins** and **ends**, and how the poem's message **develops**.

Think about language and imagery

1) Analyse the **language** — think about **why** the poet has chosen certain **words** and **language techniques**.

2) Look out for different types of **imagery** — language that creates a **picture in your mind**:

- **Personification** — describing a **nonliving thing** as if it has **human thoughts** and **feelings**, or **behaves** in a human way.
- **Metaphors** — describing things by saying that **they are something else**.
- **Similes** — describing things by **comparing** them to something else, usually using the words "like" or "as".

3) **Think about** the **effect** of the language and imagery on the reader — consider how it makes you **feel**.

Five Steps to Analysing the Unseen Poems

Look out for poetic devices

1) Poets use **poetic devices** for **effect** in their writing — here are some **examples**, but there are **lots more**:

- **Punctuation** (e.g. caesurae, enjambment, end-stopped lines) affects the poem's **pace** and how it **flows**.
- **Repetition** often **reinforces** a key point or idea.
- **Contrasts** can **emphasise** key ideas or create a **sense of balance**.
- **Sound effects** (e.g. onomatopoeia, sibilance, alliteration, assonance) can create a particular mood or **atmosphere**, **highlight** important ideas or **reflect events** in the poem.
- **Appeals to the senses** create a **vivid** impression by engaging different senses.

> Look up any terms you don't know in the glossary at the back of this book.

2) As with everything you pick out of a poem, it's **really important** that you don't just say what the technique is — you also need to **comment** on the **effect** that it has.

5) Include your thoughts and feelings about the poem

1) Examiners love to hear what *you think* of a poem and how it makes *you feel* — giving a **personal response** will make your answer **original** and help it to **stand out** from the crowd.

2) Think about how well the poem gets its **message** across and what **impact** it has on you.

3) Try **not** to use "**I**" though. Don't say "I felt sad that the narrator's brother died" — it's much **better** to say "It makes the reader feel the narrator's sense of sadness at the death of his brother."

4) Think about any **other ways** that the poem could be **interpreted** — if a poem is a bit **ambiguous**, or you think that a particular line or phrase could have several **different meanings**, then **say so**.

Take your analysis further to get a grade 9

There's no single way to get **top marks**, but these points can help take your analysis to the **next level**:

1) Treat the poem as a **conscious creation** — every **word** or **technique** has been **deliberately chosen** by the poet. Show that you understand this by writing about **what** the **poet** does and **why**:

- **Think carefully** about the poem and analyse in **real depth** the ways the poet creates meaning.
- Pick out **individual words** and **phrases** that are rich in meaning, then explore their **effect** in detail.
- Consider whether there could be **different interpretations** of the poem and comment on them.

2) Develop a **clear argument** and **build your essay** around it. **Link** each paragraph of your answer to your **argument** so that you **really answer the question** in the exam.

3) Remember that the examiners value **quality over quantity** — make a few **highly detailed** and **relevant** points, rather than attempting to write about the whole poem.

Think about the five steps when you analyse a poem...

You could even come up with a cheeky acrostic to help you remember them. Let's see... **S**ubject, **M**essage, **M**ood, **T**echniques, **P**ersonal Response — **S**melly **M**ackerel **M**ostly **T**astes **P**retty **R**ank. Winner.

How to Write a Good Answer

Now you know **what** to write about, it's time for some advice on **how** to write about it. Happy days.

Read each question carefully and plan your answers

1) Make sure that you're **familiar** with the **format** of the two **questions**. For **Question 1**, you have to **analyse** one unseen poem, and **Question 2** asks you to **compare** that poem with another one.

2) **Read the questions** carefully — **underline** the **key words** and refer back to them as you write.

3) **Get to grips** with the poem and get a sense of its **message** and **key features** before planning your answer.

4) Write a **short plan** that covers your main points (see **page 9** for more on planning).

Get to the point straight away in your introduction

1) Your **introduction** should begin by **clearly** laying out your **answer** to the question in a sentence or two.

2) Try to use **words** or **phrases** from the **question** in your introduction — this will show the examiner that you're **answering the question**.

3) Use the rest of the introduction to give a **brief overview** of how the poem or poems present the **theme** given in the question — include the **main ideas** from your **plan**, but **save** the **evidence** for later.

4) Keep your introduction nice and **short** — most of your **marks** will come from the **main body** of the essay.

Use the main body of your essay to develop your argument

1) The **main body** of your essay should be roughly three to five paragraphs that **develop** your argument.

2) Make sure each of your points is **linked** to the question and follows a **clear** central **argument**.

3) A good way to do this is to start each paragraph with a **clear point** or **opening statement** that directly connects the poem or poems back to the question.

4) You can use P.E.E.D. to structure your paragraphs. **P.E.E.D.** stands for: Point, Example, Explain, Develop.

> **POINT** — Begin each paragraph by making a **point**.
> **EXAMPLE** — Then give an **example** from the poem.
> **EXPLAIN** — Explain **how** the example **supports** your opening point.
> **DEVELOP** — Finish the paragraph by **developing** your point further.

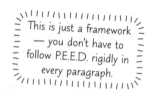
This is just a framework — you don't have to follow P.E.E.D. rigidly in every paragraph.

5) You can develop your points in a **variety** of ways — here are some ideas:

- **Explain** the **effect** on the reader.
- **Analyse** the **language** more closely.
- **Link** to **another part** of the poem.
- Give an **alternative interpretation** of your example.

6) **Question 2** is a **comparison** question, so your answer needs to be structured differently to Question 1:

- You could **compare** the poems in **each paragraph** by writing about a **feature** of **one poem** and **explaining** how the **other poem** is similar or different.
- Alternatively, you could write about **one poem at a time** — you could write about different elements of **one poem**, then write about **the other**, **comparing** it with the first poem.

How to Write a Good Answer

Use details from the text to back up your points

1) You need to **back up your ideas** with **quotes** from or **references** to the poems. Here are some **tips**:

- **Choose** your quotes **carefully** — they have to be **relevant** to the point you're making.
- **Don't** quote **large chunks** of text — keep quotes **short** and cut out anything unnecessary.
- **Embed** quotes into your sentences — this means **placing** them **smoothly** and **naturally** into your writing, e.g. 'The poet describes the path as "<u>grassy</u>" and covered in "<u>leaves</u>".'
- **Explain** your quotes — you need to use them as **evidence** to support your **argument**.

2) Here's an **example** of how to **use quotes** in your answers, and what to **avoid**:

> ✗ The narrator describes how they chose the second path because it seemed slightly less well-trodden than the first — "Because it was grassy and wanted wear; / Though as for that the passing there / Had worn them really about the same".
>
> ✓ The narrator chose the second path because it "wanted wear". This suggests that they wished to be different, despite acknowledging that the paths were "about the same".

This quote is too long and it doesn't fit into the sentence structure.

These quotes are nicely embedded into the sentence.

3) **Quotes** are usually the **clearest** way to illustrate a point, but sometimes you can use a **paraphrased detail instead** — e.g. if you need to describe one of the **writer's techniques** or one of the **poem's features**.

4) **Don't** write a **lengthy explanation** of what happens in the poem — keep any references **brief** and **relevant**.

Use sophisticated language and relevant technical terms

1) Your writing has to sound **sophisticated** and **stylish**. It should be **concise** and **accurate**, with no **vague words** or **waffle**.

2) You should use an **impressive range** of **vocabulary**. Don't keep using the **same word** to describe something — instead, try to **vary** how you say things.

Use the glossary at the back of this book to learn technical terms which you could use in the exam.

3) To get top marks, you need to use the **correct technical terms** when you're writing about poetry.

4) However, make sure you **only** use words that you know the **meaning** of. For example, don't say that a poem has a 'volta' if you don't know what it **really means** — it will be **obvious** to the examiner.

5) It's **not enough** to just **name** a feature — you need to explain the **effect** that it has on the reader.

Your conclusion must answer the question

1) **Finish** each essay with a **conclusion** — this should **summarise** your **answer** to the question.

2) It's also your **last chance** to **impress** the examiner, so make your final sentence **memorable**. You could **develop** your **opinion** of the poem(s), or **highlight** the **features** that best **support** your argument.

Always support your arguments with evidence...

If I've said it once, I've said it a thousand times (as my mum likes to say — I'm not too sure what it means). Back up each point with quotes or examples from the poems, otherwise you'll miss out on easy marks.

Question 1 — Analysing One Poem

Question 1 will ask you to analyse **one** of the unseen poems. **Read** the question carefully and underline the **key words**, then use the advice on the previous page to **annotate** the poem and pick out the important bits.

Here's a sample exam Question 1

You need to write about the techniques the poet uses, e.g. **form**, **structure** and **language**.

Q1 In 'The Road Not Taken', <u>how</u> does Robert Frost explore <u>life choices</u> and <u>how they affect people</u>?   **(24 marks)**

It's asking 'what's the poem's **message** about **life choices** and the **effects** of choices?'

This is how you might annotate the first poem

Read through the poem, and **mark** any bits of it that **stand out**.
Jot down your thoughts too — it'll help you **plan** your essay (see p.9).

Annotate your poem in any way that works for you — underline, highlight or scribble notes.

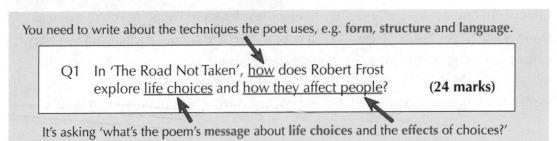

Subject — the narrator tries something new and takes a different route.

Setting — autumn.

The Road Not Taken

First-person narrator.

Extended metaphor — splitting of the road represents difficult life choices.

Two roads diverged in a yellow wood,
And sorry I could not travel both
And be one traveler, long I stood
And looked down one as far as I could
To where it bent in the undergrowth;

Caesura indicates a pause.

Repetition hints at narrator's indecision.

Form — ABAAB rhyme scheme reflects narrator's indecisiveness.

5

Then took the other, as just as fair,
And having perhaps the better claim,
Because it was grassy and wanted wear;
Though as for that the passing there
Had worn them really about the same,

Both paths seem just as nice.

Structure — sudden change of heart.

Alliteration.

10

And both that morning equally lay
In leaves no step had trodden black.
Oh, I kept the first for another day!
Yet knowing how way leads on to way,
I doubted if I should ever come back.

Almost impossible to distinguish between the two paths.

Exclamation mark adds emphasis to the line.

Narrator tries to convince themselves that they can still return to the other path.

15

Feelings — regret, anxiety.

Sibilance emphasises the narrator sighing.

I shall be telling this with a sigh
Somewhere ages and ages hence:
Two roads diverged in a wood, and I—
I took the one less traveled by,
And that has made all the difference.

Feelings — a sigh can suggest either nostalgia or remorse.

Dash indicates hesitation.

Cyclical structure.

20

Ambiguous conclusion — could be either positive or negative.

Robert Frost

Worked Answer

After **reading** and **annotating** the poem, you should have a better idea of the **message** the poet is trying to get across and how you might answer the **question**. Before answering it, spend some time making an **essay plan**.

Spend five minutes planning your answer

1) Always **plan** your answer **before** you start — this will help you to focus all of your **ideas** on the question.

2) Focus on **three or four key quotes** from the poem.

3) Remember to write about **what** the poet says and **how** they say it.

4) **Don't** spend **too long** on your plan. It's only **rough work**, so you don't need to write in full sentences.

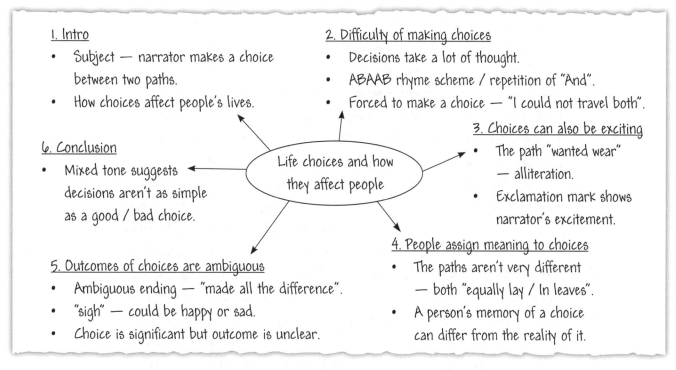

1. Intro
- Subject — narrator makes a choice between two paths.
- How choices affect people's lives.

6. Conclusion
- Mixed tone suggests decisions aren't as simple as a good / bad choice.

5. Outcomes of choices are ambiguous
- Ambiguous ending — "made all the difference".
- "sigh" — could be happy or sad.
- Choice is significant but outcome is unclear.

Life choices and how they affect people

2. Difficulty of making choices
- Decisions take a lot of thought.
- ABAAB rhyme scheme / repetition of "And".
- Forced to make a choice — "I could not travel both".

3. Choices can also be exciting
- The path "wanted wear" — alliteration.
- Exclamation mark shows narrator's excitement.

4. People assign meaning to choices
- The paths aren't very different — both "equally lay / In leaves".
- A person's memory of a choice can differ from the reality of it.

5) Once you've got a **plan** for your essay, you're ready to tackle Question 1.
I've written an answer for you this time, but don't expect to see me in your exam...

This is how you could answer Question 1

Use your essay plan to make sure you answer the question.

'The Road Not Taken' explores life choices and how they affect people. Robert Frost uses the extended metaphor of a fork in the road to symbolise the choices people face and how they ultimately must make a decision. He uses alliteration and repetition, as well as aspects of form and structure, to present both the difficulty of choices in life and the impact these choices have on people.

The narrator shows the difficulty of making choices when they are stood facing the fork in the road. The narrator's hesitation is revealed by the repetition of "And" in the first stanza, which suggests they are weighing up the choice between the two paths, but also through the ABAAB rhyme scheme, which reflects how the narrator considers both choices, then switches back and forth between the two. Through this use of form, the poet could be suggesting that decisions take a lot of time and thought.

Clear start, mentioning the main theme of the poem.

Write about the poem's main messages early on in your essay.

Comment on form and the effect it has.

This answer continues on page 10.

Section One — Exam Advice

10

Worked Answer

The narrator's choice reflects choices the reader may have faced in that, when the narrator looks down the path "as far" as they could, the reader is reminded of times they may have weighed up the advantages and disadvantages of a choice before making it.

Although choices are presented as difficult, the possibilities they provide are also presented as exciting. The narrator seems to show excitement at the prospect of taking the path that "wanted wear". This sense of excitement is emphasised through the alliteration of the 'w' sound, as it gives the reader the impression that the narrator is eager to be the person who wears it down. The use of the exclamation mark in "Oh, I kept the first for another day!" further reflects this excitement, as it implies that the narrator already looks forward to the possibility of returning to try the other path.

One interpretation of the poem is that people assign meaning to the choices they make. The image of the paths which "equally lay / In leaves no step had trodden black" shows that the paths are practically identical. Despite this, the narrator imagines themselves saying that they "took the one less traveled by", suggesting that perhaps a person's memory of making a choice can differ from the reality.

This assigning of meaning could be to justify a choice, as people sometimes question or regret the choices they make. This idea is presented in the poem through the use of a first-person voice. This gives lines tinged with regret, such as "I doubted if I should ever come back", even more emotion. Furthermore, a cyclical structure is created through the repetition of the phrase "Two roads diverged" in the first and final stanzas. This reflects how the narrator looks back on the decision they made and perhaps suggests that they keep questioning their choice.

Frost presents the outcome of the narrator's choice as ambiguous. The narrator ends the poem by imagining that their choice "made all the difference". However, it's not clear whether this "difference" has been positive or negative. This feeling of ambiguity is emphasised through the use of the word "sigh", as although the narrator could be sighing with a sense of nostalgia, it could also be seen in a negative light. In this way, Frost highlights how, although choices have consequences, the nature of these consequences can be ambiguous, perhaps reflecting how people are often unsure whether or not they have made the right choice.

By using the extended metaphor of a fork in the road, Frost explores the intricacies of making a choice and the impact these decisions have on people. The poem is punctuated with moments of decision, indecision, excitement and regret, which gives the poem a mixed tone that reflects how life choices affect people differently. The poet chooses to leave the poem open to interpretation, which gives the reader the impression that choices in life and the impact they have are often unclear.

Annotations (margin notes):

- Comment on how aspects of the poem affect the reader.
- Mention any poetic devices that you spot.
- Think about different interpretations to help you get top marks.
- Write about feelings and mood, and use quotes to back up your points.
- Sum up the _what_ and _how_ in your final paragraph.
- Mention specific language features and explain why the poet used them.
- Write about any imagery in the poem.
- Comment on structure and the effect it has.
- Always use quotes to back up points.
- Give a personal response to the poem.

EXAM TIP

Make sure you proofread your answers...

The examiner won't be very impressed if your answers don't have good spelling, punctuation and grammar. Always give yourself a couple of minutes at the end of the exam to read back over what you've written.

Section One — Exam Advice

Question 2 — Comparing Two Poems

One down, one to go. Things get a little trickier here as you'll have to **compare two poems**.
Treat yourself to a little break, then read through the **following advice** on how to tackle **Question 2**.

Question 2 will ask you about two poems

1) **Question 2** will ask you to **compare** the **two unseen poems**. This means that you
need to write about the **similarities** and **differences** between them.

2) This question is about the **techniques** the poets use and their **effect on the reader**,
so focus on the **structure, form** and **language** used in the two poems.

3) Remember, Question 2 is **only** worth **8 marks**, so **don't spend too long** on your answer — you just
need to make **three or four** clear points and back them up with **examples** from the poems.

Four steps to answering Question 2

- **Don't** be tempted to start writing **without thinking** about what you're going to say.

- Instead, use this handy **four-step plan** to quickly **organise your thoughts**
and write an answer that'll knock the examiner's socks off:

1) **Read** the question carefully and underline the **key words**.

2) **Annotate** the second poem, focusing on the **techniques** used and how they
affect the reader (see pages 3-5). Think about **similarities and differences**
between these techniques and those used in the first poem.

3) **Plan** your answer. Identify **three or four** key **similarities and/or differences**
that you are going to write about.

4) **Write** your answer. Use your plan to make sure that **every paragraph** discusses
one similarity or difference between the **techniques** used in the two poems.

Here's a sample exam Question 2

Before you start annotating the second poem, **read** the question carefully
and make sure that you **understand** exactly what you're being asked to do.

> Q2 'The Road Not Taken' and 'Midnight on the Great Western' both feature
> <u>journeys that can be seen to represent life</u>. <u>Compare</u> the <u>methods</u>
> used to present these journeys in the two poems.   **(8 marks)**

This is the **theme**.

You need to **compare** the poets' techniques, e.g.
form, structure and **language**, in the two poems.

Remember to stick to the question...

You should always keep the question in mind when you plan and write your answer. It's easy to go off on a
tangent, but sadly you won't pick up marks if your points are irrelevant — no matter how brilliant they are.

Worked Answer

After completing Question 1, you'll be ready to get stuck into **Question 2**. You'll need to make **another plan** for this question, so think about any **similarities** and **differences** between the two poems while annotating.

This is how you might annotate the second poem

Read through the poem, and **mark** the most important bits. Remember, in your essay you need to write about the **form**, **structure** and **language** used in the poem and the **effect** they have on the reader.

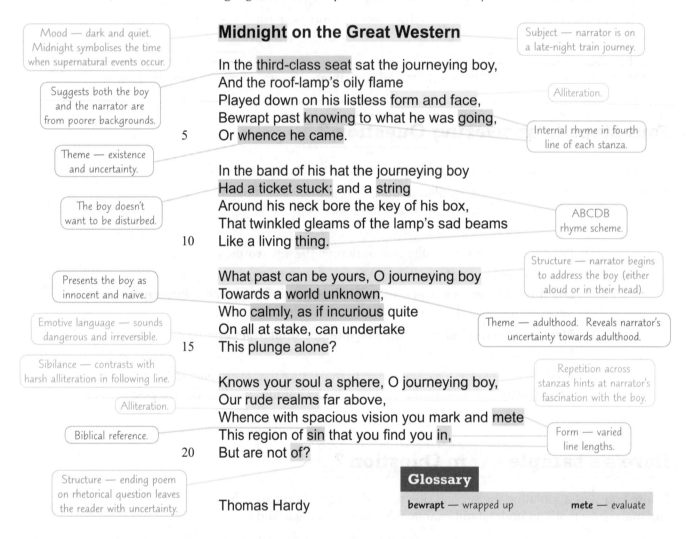

Mood — dark and quiet. Midnight symbolises the time when supernatural events occur.

Suggests both the boy and the narrator are from poorer backgrounds.

Theme — existence and uncertainty.

The boy doesn't want to be disturbed.

Presents the boy as innocent and naive.

Emotive language — sounds dangerous and irreversible.

Sibilance — contrasts with harsh alliteration in following line.

Alliteration.

Biblical reference.

Structure — ending poem on rhetorical question leaves the reader with uncertainty.

Subject — narrator is on a late-night train journey.

Alliteration.

Internal rhyme in fourth line of each stanza.

ABCDB rhyme scheme.

Structure — narrator begins to address the boy (either aloud or in their head).

Theme — adulthood. Reveals narrator's uncertainty towards adulthood.

Repetition across stanzas hints at narrator's fascination with the boy.

Form — varied line lengths.

Midnight on the Great Western

In the third-class seat sat the journeying boy,
And the roof-lamp's oily flame
Played down on his listless form and face,
Bewrapt past knowing to what he was going,
5   Or whence he came.

In the band of his hat the journeying boy
Had a ticket stuck; and a string
Around his neck bore the key of his box,
That twinkled gleams of the lamp's sad beams
10   Like a living thing.

What past can be yours, O journeying boy
Towards a world unknown,
Who calmly, as if incurious quite
On all at stake, can undertake
15   This plunge alone?

Knows your soul a sphere, O journeying boy,
Our rude realms far above,
Whence with spacious vision you mark and mete
This region of sin that you find you in,
20   But are not of?

Thomas Hardy

Glossary

bewrapt — wrapped up   **mete** — evaluate

This is how you could plan your answer

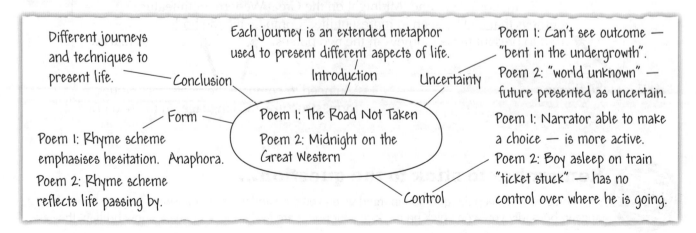

Different journeys and techniques to present life.

Each journey is an extended metaphor used to present different aspects of life.

Poem 1: Can't see outcome — "bent in the undergrowth".
Poem 2: "world unknown" — future presented as uncertain.

Conclusion   Introduction   Uncertainty

Form

Poem 1: Rhyme scheme emphasises hesitation. Anaphora.
Poem 2: Rhyme scheme reflects life passing by.

Poem 1: The Road Not Taken
Poem 2: Midnight on the Great Western

Poem 1: Narrator able to make a choice — is more active.
Poem 2: Boy asleep on train "ticket stuck" — has no control over where he is going.

Control

Worked Answer

Once you've **understood the question** and feel like you've **got to grips with the poems**, it's time to start writing. When writing your essay for **Question 2**, always make sure you're **comparing both poems**.

This is how you could answer Question 2

> 'The Road Not Taken' and 'Midnight on the Great Western' both present different journeys — one a walk in the woods, the other a train journey. Both of these journeys can be seen as extended metaphors for life. The poets use symbolism as well as aspects of form and structure to present these journeys and, by extension, life.
>
> Both poems present life as being uncertain. In 'The Road Not Taken', the narrator couldn't see the end of the path because it "bent in the undergrowth". This emphasises the narrator's feeling of uncertainty because the outcome of their choice isn't clear. The use of the word "bent" implies a sharp and sudden lack of path, making the uncertainty seem even more intimidating to the reader. Life is also presented as being uncertain in 'Midnight on the Great Western', when the boy is described as heading towards a "world unknown". A reader can interpret this 'world' as adulthood, and by using this metaphor, the poet emphasises just how much uncertainty there is in the boy's future, because the vastness of a "world" suggests that there is nowhere the boy can go to escape uncertainty.
>
> The poems suggest that despite this uncertainty, people have varying levels of control in life. In 'The Road Not Taken', the narrator has an active role in their journey through the wood. They are able to choose between paths and even change their mind when they "took the other". In contrast, the figures in 'Midnight on the Great Western' are aboard a moving train, literally set on tracks that they cannot deviate from. This lack of control is emphasised as the boy is asleep and "journeying" with a "ticket stuck" in his hat. This presents him as a passive figure with no control over his destination — he simply has to go wherever the journey takes him.
>
> The irregular forms of both poems reflect these ideas. The ABAAB rhyme scheme in 'The Road Not Taken' bounces between the 'A' and 'B' rhymes to reflect how the narrator is uncertain of their choice. This uncertainty is reinforced by the anaphora of "And" in the first stanza, as it suggests the narrator can't decide which path to take. In contrast, the ABCDB rhyme scheme in 'Midnight on the Great Western' emphasises the passengers' lack of control. The 'ABCD' lines reflect the forward momentum of the train, how it cannot deviate from its set course and how the passengers have no control over where it goes. However, the return of the 'B' rhyme in the final line of each stanza reminds the reader of life's uncertainty.
>
> Although the journeys in 'The Road Not Taken' and 'Midnight on the Great Western' show narrators with contrasting degrees of control, both poets use aspects of language, structure and form, in particular the use of rhyme scheme, to show how these journeys represent the uncertainty of life.

Annotations (left margin):
- Introduce your paragraphs with a comparison.
- Remember to compare the two poems.
- Compare the form of the two poems.
- Explain how the techniques in the poems affect the reader.

Annotations (right margin):
- Show that you've understood the question.
- Use quotes to support your argument.
- Show that you understand poetic devices in the poems.
- Sum up the similarities and differences in your conclusion.

Organise your time wisely in the exam...

EXAM TIP There's a lot to do for the Unseen Poetry section and not a huge amount of time to do it, so you'll need to think about how to manage your time. Question 1 is worth a lot more marks, so spend more time on it.

Tattoos

Brian Patten was born in Liverpool in 1946. He became well known in the 1960s for his efforts to make poetry **accessible** to **wider audiences**. Many of his poems have been **translated** into various **other languages**.

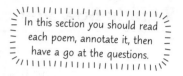

In this section you should read each poem, annotate it, then have a go at the questions.

Tattoos

No doubt in her youth
The many tattoos on my grandmother's arms
Were bold and clear:
No grave-marks or burst blood vessels sullied
5   the breast of the blue-bird that flew
               upwards from her wrist-bone;
On her biceps
The sails on the three-decked galleon were not yellow or
          wrinkled,
10   And each angry thorn on the blue-stemmed rose was
               needle-sharp,
Its folded petals unblurred by time.
A child, I studied those tattoos intently —
Back then they seemed as mysterious as runes to me.
15   But all those tribal decorations went the way of her own
               bravado.
Ageing, the colours faded,
And her world shrank to a small island in the brain,
A tumour on which memory was shipwrecked
20   Till finally that galleon came to rest
One fathom down beneath Liverpool clay,
Its sails deflated, the blue-bird mute,
The rose gone to seed.

Brian Patten

Glossary

sullied — spoiled the quality of
galleon — a large sailing ship
runes — can mean either the letters of ancient alphabets, or small, magical rocks / pieces of bone
one fathom — a unit of length measuring six feet (usually used for water depth)

Brian Patten

Read and annotate the poem on page 14, then answer these questions. It's good practice to make a quick plan for each exam-style question too. After you've done all that, give yourself a Patten the back...

Warm-up Questions

1) Briefly explain what you think the poem is about.

2) What is the effect of the poem being written from the grandchild's point of view rather than from the point of view of the grandmother?

3) Briefly describe the emotions that the poet puts across. How does the poet show these emotions?

4) What do the grandmother's fading tattoos represent?

5) Why do you think the poet included language associated with sailing?

6) What does the word "bravado" suggest about the grandmother's character?

7) How do you think the narrator feels about their grandmother ageing?

8) Briefly describe the form of the poem. What effect does this form have?

Focus on... Imagery

Imagery is any language that paints a picture in your mind. It includes metaphors and similes.

1) a) Find an example of a simile in the poem.

   b) What is the effect of this?

2) What does the metaphor "memory was shipwrecked" suggest about the narrator's grandmother?

3) What idea do you think the poet is trying to convey by having the galleon end up "One fathom down beneath Liverpool clay"?

Exam-style Question — Part 1

What do you think the narrator is saying about their grandmother? How are these ideas presented?

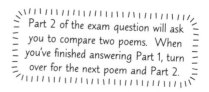
Part 2 of the exam question will ask you to compare two poems. When you've finished answering Part 1, turn over for the next poem and Part 2.

The Ageing Schoolmaster

Vernon Scannell was born in Lincolnshire, in 1922. He served in the army during the **Second World War** before becoming a **teacher** in the 1950s. His poems often centre around the theme of **mortality**.

The Ageing Schoolmaster

And now another autumn morning finds me
With chalk dust on my sleeve and in my breath,
Preoccupied with vague, habitual speculation
On the huge inevitability of death.

5   Not wholly wretched, yet knowing absolutely
That I shall never reacquaint myself with joy,
I sniff the smell of ink and chalk and my mortality
And think of when I rolled, a gormless boy,

And rollicked round the playground of my hours,
10   And wonder when precisely tolled the bell
Which summoned me from summer liberties
And brought me to this chill autumnal cell

From which I gaze upon the april faces
That gleam before me, like apples ranged on shelves,
15   And yet I feel no pinch or prick of envy
Nor would I have them know their sentenced selves.

With careful effort I can separate the faces,
The dull, the clever, the various shapes and sizes,
But in the autumn shades I find I only
20   Brood upon death, who carries off all the prizes.

Vernon Scannell

Even the pupils found the prospect of double chemistry unappeeling.

Vernon Scannell

This is the **second poem** in the pair. Soon, it will be time to **compare** it with the first poem, just like you will in the exam. Before you start comparing them though, **familiarise** yourself with these **warm-up questions**.

Warm-up Questions

1) Explain what the poem is about in a sentence or two.

2) How would you describe the mood in the second stanza? How does the poet create this mood?

3) Do you think the narrator would like to be a "boy" again? Explain your answer.

4) Read the second stanza. Find an example of where the poet uses language that appeals to the senses and explain its effect.

5) Give one example of a simile used in the poem. What effect does it have?

6) What do you think the poet is trying to say about:
   a) youth   b) getting older   c) death

7) How does the poet use rhyme in this poem? What effect does this have?

8) Identify one example of personification in the poem. What effect does it have on the reader?

Focus on... Vocabulary

Vocabulary is the specific words the poet uses. If a poem uses a group of words that all have a similar theme, this set of words is called a 'semantic field' — for example, this poem uses the semantic field of seasons. This can help to create a particular mood or tone, or to emphasise certain ideas.

1) What does the first line "And now another autumn morning finds me" suggest about the narrator?

2) What could the poet be referring to when he writes "this chill autumnal cell" in line 12?

3) Why do you think the poet uses the semantic field of seasons in this poem?

Exam-style Question — Part 2

The narrators of 'Tattoos' and 'The Ageing Schoolmaster' consider the effects of getting older. Compare the methods used to present attitudes towards ageing in the poems.

Originally

Carol Ann Duffy was born in Glasgow in 1955. She was the first woman and first Scottish person to be named **Poet Laureate**. Her poem, 'Originally', describes her **childhood experience** of moving to England.

Originally

We came from our own country in a red room
which fell through the fields, our mother singing
our father's name to the turn of the wheels.
My brothers cried, one of them bawling, *Home,*
5   *Home*, as the miles rushed back to the city,
the street, the house, the vacant rooms
where we didn't live any more. I stared
at the eyes of a blind toy, holding its paw.

All childhood is an emigration. Some are slow,
10   leaving you standing, resigned, up an avenue
where no one you know stays. Others are sudden.
Your accent wrong. Corners, which seem familiar,
leading to unimagined pebble-dashed estates, big boys
eating worms and shouting words you don't understand.
15   My parents' anxiety stirred like a loose tooth
in my head. *I want our own country*, I said.

But then you forget, or don't recall, or change,
and, seeing your brother swallow a slug, feel only
a skelf of shame. I remember my tongue
20   shedding its skin like a snake, my voice
in the classroom sounding just like the rest. Do I only think
I lost a river, culture, speech, sense of first space
and the right place? Now, *Where do you come from?*
strangers ask. *Originally?* And I hesitate.

Carol Ann Duffy

Glossary

skelf — Scottish dialect word that means a splinter or small piece of wood

Carol Ann Duffy

Originally, we wanted a page of cute dogs photos here, but these **practice questions** will be more useful.
Make **notes** on the page as you do them — it'll make it much easier to do the **exam-style questions** later.

Warm-up Questions

1) Briefly explain what you think the poem is about.

2) What is the effect of the repetition of "*Home*" in the first stanza?

3) What is suggested by the sentence "All childhood is an emigration."?

4) What is the effect of the end-stopping in the sentence "Others are sudden."?

5) Why do you think the poet used the word "skelf" in line 19?

6) Identify one simile in the poem. Why do you think the poet has used it?

7) What is the effect of the poet's use of direct speech in the poem?

8) What do you notice about the use of rhyme in the poem?
   How does this reflect the events in the poem?

9) Do you think the narrator is sure of her identity by the end of the poem?

Focus on... Mood

The mood of the poem is the feeling or atmosphere it creates for the reader. Poets can use lots of techniques to create mood, including language, rhythm and narrative voice.

1) a) What do you think the general mood is in the first stanza?

   b) How does the poet create this mood?

2) How does the poet create a feeling of confusion in the second stanza?

3) a) What mood do the questions in the third stanza create?

   b) How do they do this?

Exam-style Question — Part 1

What do you think the narrator is saying about moving to a new place?
How does the poet convey the narrator's feelings about moving?

Hard Water

Jean Sprackland was born in Burton upon Trent, in the Midlands, in 1962. 'Hard Water', published in 2003, was inspired by Burton — a town famous for its **breweries**, which use the **local hard water** to brew the beer.

Hard Water

I tried the soft stuff on holiday in Wales,
a mania of teadrinking and hairwashing,
excitable soap which never rinsed away,

but I loved coming home to this.
5   Flat. Straight. Like the vowels,
like the straight talk: *hey up me duck*.
I'd run the tap with its swimming-pool smell,
get it cold and anaesthetic. Stand the glass
and let the little fizz of anxiety settle.
10   Honest water, bright and not quite clean.
The frankness of limestone, of gypsum,
the sour steam of cooling towers,
the alchemical taste of brewing.

On pitiless nights, I had to go for the bus
15   before last orders. I'd turn up my face,
let rain scald my eyelids and lips.
It couldn't lie. Fell thick
with a payload of acid. No salt –
this rain had forgotten the sea.
20   I opened my mouth, speaking nothing
in spite of my book-learning.
I let a different cleverness wash my tongue.
It tasted of work, the true taste
of early mornings, the blunt taste
25   of *don't get mardy*, of *too bloody deep for me*,
fierce lovely water that marked me for life
as belonging, regardless.

Jean Sprackland

Glossary

hard water — water containing lots of minerals
gypsum — a type of mineral
alchemical — being related to alchemy (the medieval science of changing
        things that aren't worth anything into something valuable)
mardy — dialect word for grumpy or sulky

'What do you want?'

Jean Sprackland

A few **warm-up questions** should help turn this hard water into soft water. Then have a go at the **exam-style question** below — keep flicking back to 'Originally' on page 18 to make sure you haven't missed anything.

Warm-up Questions

1) Explain what the poem is about in a sentence or two.

2) Describe the form of the poem. What effect does it have?

3) How does the tone of the poem change at the start of the second stanza?

4) What is the effect of the line "Flat. Straight. Like the vowels," (line 5)?

5) What technique does the poet use to compare the hard water to the local people?

6) Find an example of sibilance in the poem and explain the effect it has.

7) What does the narrator mean by "a different cleverness" in line 22?

8) What evidence is there in the poem to suggest that the narrator is proud of where they come from?

9) What do you notice about the final line of the poem? What effect does this have?

Focus on... Voice

The voice of the poem refers to the person narrating the poem — it may be the poet themselves or a character they've created. The speaker's vocabulary and how they speak can hint at their character.

1) What effect does the use of a first-person narrator have in the poem?

2) a) Give one example of dialect that is used in the poem.

   b) Why might this dialect have been used?

Exam-style Question — Part 2

The narrators of 'Originally' and 'Hard Water' both convey their feelings towards their roots. Compare the methods used to present these feelings in the two poems.

Island Man

Grace Nichols was born in Guyana in 1950. She was a teacher and journalist in the Caribbean until she moved to Britain in 1977. Both British and Caribbean cultures and how they interlink are important to her.

Island Man

(for a Caribbean island man in London who still wakes up to the sound of the sea)

Morning
and island man wakes up
to the sound of blue surf
in his head
5   the steady breaking and wombing

wild seabirds
and fishermen pushing out to sea
the sun surfacing defiantly

from the east
10   of his small emerald island
he always comes back   groggily groggily

Comes back to sands
of a grey metallic soar
             to surge of wheels
15   to dull North Circular roar

muffling muffling
his crumpled pillow waves
island man heaves himself

Another London day

Grace Nichols

Glossary

North Circular — a busy London road

Stanley was settling in well — he
knew he'd never miss the bustling
sounds of the big city...

Grace Nichols

Once you've finished wishing you were on a Caribbean island instead of doing **unseen poetry** practice, have a go at these **questions**. When you're done, turn over the page for the **next poem**.

Warm-up Questions

1) Briefly summarise what you think the poem is about.

2) What is the effect of referring to the man in the poem as "island man"?

3) What do the lines "and island man wakes up / to the sound of blue surf / in his head" suggest about the way the man feels about his original island home?

4) What is the effect of repetition in the phrases "groggily groggily" and "muffling muffling"?

5) Describe how language relating to the sea is used to link the island and London. What effect does this have?

6) Identify an example of sibilance in the poem. What is its effect?

7) a) How does the poet use colour in the poem?

   b) How does this affect the presentation of the man's original home and London in the poem?

8) Comment on the final line of the poem, "Another London day". What effect does it have?

Focus on... Form

Form refers to the features of the poem — things like the number and length of lines, whether it's broken into stanzas, and the use of rhyme and rhythm. Poets use form to create all sorts of effects.

1) Why do you think the poem starts with the one-word line "Morning"?

2) What is the effect of enjambment in the poem?

3) Why do you think the poet chose to add extra spacing before "groggily groggily" and "to surge of wheels"?

Exam-style Question — Part 1

What does the speaker suggest about life in the Caribbean compared to life in London? How does the poet put these ideas across?

Remember

Joy Harjo was born in Oklahoma in 1951. She is a poet and musician of Native American descent.
A lot of her writing explores Native American culture and beliefs, as well as the effects of colonialism.

Remember

Remember the sky that you were born under,
know each of the star's stories.
Remember the moon, know who she is.
Remember the sun's birth at dawn, that is the
5   strongest point of time. Remember sundown
and the giving away to night.
Remember your birth, how your mother struggled
to give you form and breath. You are evidence of
her life, and her mother's, and hers.
10   Remember your father. He is your life, also.
Remember the earth whose skin you are:
red earth, black earth, yellow earth, white earth
brown earth, we are earth.
Remember the plants, trees, animal life who all have their
15   tribes, their families, their histories, too. Talk to them,
listen to them. They are alive poems.
Remember the wind. Remember her voice. She knows the
origin of this universe.
Remember you are all people and all people
20   are you.
Remember you are this universe and this
universe is you.
Remember all is in motion, is growing, is you.
Remember language comes from this.
25   Remember the dance language is, that life is.
Remember.

Joy Harjo

Joy Harjo

Remember to **read** the poem, remember to **annotate** the poem, remember to... well, you get the picture. Have a bash at these zingy **warm-up questions** before you tackle the **exam-style question**.

Warm-up Questions

1) Explain briefly what you think the poem is about.

2) What do the first two lines, "Remember the sky that you were born under, / know each of the star's stories", suggest about how a person should think about their own life?

3) Why do you think the poet chose to use second-person address in the poem? Explain your answer.

4) What is the effect of the poem being written as one continuous stanza?

5) Find an example of enjambment in the poem and explain its effect.

6) Give an example of personification in the poem and explain why it is used by the poet.

7) Find an example of a metaphor in the poem. Explain what effect it creates.

8) How would you describe the overall mood of the poem? Explain your answer.

Focus on... Repetition

Poets often repeat particular words or phrases to make them stand out. This can have different effects on the reader, for example by creating a strong rhythm or strengthening a poem's message.

1) What is the effect of the repetition of "Remember" throughout the poem?

2) a) Find another example of repetition in the poem.

   b) What is the effect of the example you gave?

Exam-style Question — Part 2

Memory is important to the narrators of 'Island Man' and 'Remember'. Compare the ways the poets present their ideas in the two poems.

Crossing the Bar

Alfred Tennyson was the British **Poet Laureate** for 40 years up until his death in 1892. This poem was published **3 years** before his death and Tennyson wanted it to appear as the **final poem** in his collections.

Crossing the Bar

Sunset and evening star
    And one clear call for me!
And may there be no moaning of the bar,
    When I put out to sea,

5   But such a tide as moving seems asleep,
    Too full for sound and foam,
When that which drew from out the boundless deep
    Turns again home.

Twilight and evening bell,
10   And after that the dark!
And may there be no sadness of farewell,
    When I embark;

For though from out our bourne of Time and Place
    The flood may bear me far,
15   I hope to see my Pilot face to face
    When I have crossed the bar.

Alfred Tennyson

Glossary

bar — short for sandbar (a raised area of sand created by the movement of waves)
bourne — can mean a small stream, a destination or a boundary

Alfred Tennyson

Pretty touching stuff — you can see why he was named Poet Laureate. Here are a few more questions — once you've found your sea legs, set about tackling the exam-style question at the bottom of the page.

Warm-up Questions

1) Briefly describe what you think the poem is about.

2) Why do you think the poet chose to set the poem during "Sunset"?

3) a) What poetic technique does the poet use in the phrase "no moaning of the bar"?

   b) What does this suggest about the narrator's feelings?

4) Do you think the idea of 'crossing the bar' is an effective metaphor? Explain your answer.

5) What does the repetition of the word "When" suggest about the narrator?

6) What does the verb "hope" reveal about the narrator's attitude to death?

7) Who do you think the narrator refers to when they say "my Pilot"? What effect does this have?

8) Would you describe the poem as a religious poem? Explain your answer.

Focus on... Rhyme and Rhythm

Poets can rhyme words at the end of lines, or within lines. This can add emphasis to certain words and affect the rhythm of the poem. In turn, the rhythm affects the impact the poem has on the reader.

1) a) What rhyme scheme does the poem use?

   b) Why might the poet have chosen this form?

2) a) Describe the rhythm of the poem.

   b) What effect does it have on the reader?

Exam-style Question — Part 1

What does the poem suggest about the narrator's emotions when considering death? How does the poet put these ideas across?

Because I could not stop for Death

Another poem about death — joy. Emily Dickinson (1830-1886) was an American poet whose work is often **centred around death**. She was very **introverted** and many of her poems were only published after she died.

Because I could not stop for Death

Because I could not stop for Death –
He kindly stopped for me –
The Carriage held but just Ourselves –
And Immortality.

5   We slowly drove – He knew no haste
And I had put away
My labor and my leisure too,
For His Civility –

We passed the School, where Children strove
10   At Recess – in the Ring –
We passed the Fields of Gazing Grain –
We passed the Setting Sun –

Or rather – He passed Us –
The Dews drew quivering and Chill –
15   For only Gossamer, my Gown –
My Tippet – only Tulle –

We paused before a House that seemed
A Swelling of the Ground –
The Roof was scarcely visible –
20   The Cornice – in the Ground –

Since then – 'tis Centuries – and yet
Feels shorter than the Day
I first surmised the Horses' Heads
Were toward Eternity –

Emily Dickinson

Glossary

recess — an American word meaning a break at school
gossamer — can mean both a thin fabric, and fine cobwebs often found on grass
tippet — a woman's scarf
tulle — a very fine, net-like fabric
cornice — the decorative border around the edge of a roof
surmised — guessed or supposed

Emily Dickinson

I'm sure you know the drill by now — a few questions to warm your bones followed by a juicy comparison question. Don't forget to **flesh out** your comparison with **quotes** from the poems. Knock 'em dead...

Warm-up Questions

1) Briefly explain what you think is happening in the poem.

2) Do you think the carriage ride is an effective extended metaphor? Explain your answer.

3) The narrator shifts from using 'I' to 'we' in the second stanza. What effect does this have?

4) Give one example of repetition in the poem. What does the repetition achieve?

5) How does the tone of the poem change in the fourth stanza? What effect does this have?

6) What does the phrase "A Swelling of the Ground" suggest about the house?

7) How is death presented in the poem? Is the presentation of death what you would expect?

8) Comment on the rhythm of the poem. What effect does it have on the reader?

9) Do you think the narrator believes in life after death? Explain your answer.

Focus on... Punctuation

Poets often use punctuation to achieve a certain effect. Caesurae, end-stopping and enjambment can change the pace of a poem and make the reader focus on particular words.

1) In the poem, the poet uses a lot of dashes. What effect does this have?

2) The poet uses just one full stop in the poem. Why do you think she chose a full stop rather than a dash in line 4?

3) What effect does the enjambment in the final stanza have?

Exam-style Question — Part 2

The narrators of 'Because I could not stop for Death' and 'Crossing the Bar' both present attitudes towards death. Compare the methods used to present these attitudes in the two poems.

My Father on His Shield

Walt McDonald was born in Texas in 1934. He served in the **United States Air Force** in the **Vietnam War** and began writing poetry around the same time. His father died in the **Second World War**.

My Father on His Shield

Shiny as wax, the cracked veneer Scotch-taped
and brittle. I can't bring my father back.
Legs crossed, he sits there brash

with a private's stripe, a world away
5   from the war they would ship him to
within days. Cannons flank his face

and banners above him like the flag
my mother kept on the mantel, folded tight,
white stars sharp-pointed on a field of blue.

10   I remember his fists, the iron he pounded,
five-pound hammer ringing steel,
the frame he made for a sled that winter

before the war. I remember the rope in his fist
around my chest, his other fist
15   shoving the snow, and downhill we dived,

his boots by my boots on the tongue,
pines whishing by, ice in my eyes, blinking
and squealing. I remember the troop train,

steam billowing like a smoke screen.
20   I remember wrecking the sled weeks later
and pounding to beat the iron flat,

but it stayed there bent
and stacked in the barn by the anvil,
and I can't bring him back.

Walt McDonald

Fumiko knew what she'd rather have flanking her face.

Glossary

smoke screen — a cloud of smoke used to hide soldiers undertaking military operations

Walt McDonald

Another sad poem *snivel* — still, I prefer it to poems about sunshine and daisies. It's time to put away the tissues and work your way through these questions. Actually, it may be best to keep the tissues to hand...

Warm-up Questions

1) Explain briefly what you think the poem is about.

2) What effect does the short sentence "I can't bring my father back." in line 2 have?

3) Describe the form of the poem. What effect does it have?

4) Why do you think the narrator's mother kept a flag "on the mantel, folded tight"?

5) Read stanzas 4 and 5. What impression do you get of the father from these stanzas?

6) Find an example of a simile in the poem and explain its effect.

7) What is the effect of the caesura in the middle of line 18?

8) Describe the mood of the final two stanzas. How does the poet create this mood?

9) What is the effect of only mentioning the father's shield in the title of the poem?

Focus on... Appeals to the Senses

It's not just how things look that matters — poets often refer to sound, smell, touch and taste to make a description more vivid or create a particular mood for the reader.

1) a) Find an example where the poet appeals to the sense of touch.
   b) What does it suggest about the narrator's memories of his father?

2) a) Which sense does the phrase "pines whishing by" appeal to?
   b) What effect does it have on the reader?

3) Why do you think the poet uses so much sensory language in the poem?

Exam-style Question — Part 1

How does the narrator feel about the loss of their father?
How does the poet present these feelings?

Those Winter Sundays

Robert Hayden (1913-1980) was born in Detroit, Michigan, and **raised by foster parents** from an early age. He rose to prominence in the **1960s** and is often regarded as one of the leading **African-American poets**.

Those Winter Sundays

Sundays too my father got up early
and put his clothes on in the blueblack cold,
then with cracked hands that ached
from labor in the weekday weather made
5   banked fires blaze. No one ever thanked him.

I'd wake and hear the cold splintering, breaking.
When the rooms were warm, he'd call,
and slowly I would rise and dress,
fearing the chronic angers of that house,

10   Speaking indifferently to him,
who had driven out the cold
and polished my good shoes as well.
What did I know, what did I know
of love's austere and lonely offices?

Robert Hayden

Glossary

offices — can mean duties or obligations as well as places of work

To keep loneliness in the office at bay, Pat and Marie would prank call their boss on her lunch hour.

Robert Hayden

Ah, at last — you're onto the **final poem** of the section. You should know your onions when it comes to **analysing poetry** by now, but just in case you need another recap: **read**, **annotate**, **plan**, **answer**. Lovely stuff.

Warm-up Questions

1) Explain briefly what you think the poem is about.

2) How does the poet create the sense that the narrator's father works hard?

3) What technique does the poet use to emphasise the short sentence "No one ever thanked him." in line 5? What effect does this have?

4) What does the phrase "Speaking indifferently to him" suggest about the communication between the narrator and their father?

5) What do you think the poet is suggesting about love in the final stanza?

6) What do the final two lines reveal about the narrator's emotions? How is this achieved?

7) How does the poet use temperature in the poem? What effect does this have?

8) The poem is loosely based on the sonnet form. Why might the poet have chosen to do this?

Focus on... Sound

Poets often choose words with a particular sound, or repeat the same sound in nearby words. These sound devices can emphasise a feeling or make a description richer.

1) a) Find an example of alliteration in the first stanza.

   b) What is the effect of this?

2) a) What sound device does the word "splintering" use?

   b) What effect does this have?

3) Explain how the poet uses sound in lines 7 and 8 to create a particular impression.

Exam-style Question — Part 2

The narrators of 'My Father on His Shield' and 'Those Winter Sundays' both present attitudes towards their fathers. Compare the way these attitudes are presented in the two poems.

Mark Scheme

This is where the fun really begins — **a whole section** where you can **mark** some **sample exam answers**. So dust off your examiner's hat, get your best red marking pen and have a good look at these **mark schemes**...

This section lets you mark some sample answer extracts

1) **Marking extracts** from sample exam answers is a **great way** to find out **exactly** what you'll need to do to get the grade you want.

2) Remember, in this section you're only marking **extracts**, not full answers. The essays you'll write in the exam will be **longer** than the answer extracts on the next few pages.

3) The **mark schemes** on these two pages are similar to the ones your **examiner** will use. The idea is for **you** to use them to help you mark the sample answer extracts in the rest of the section.

4) These extracts should give you a good idea of what the examiner will be looking for when he or she marks **your exam answer**. Don't forget, **grade 9** is the **top grade** you can get in the exam.

5) So before you do anything else, **read the mark schemes** and make sure you **understand** them.

Use this mark scheme for the answers to Question 1

Grade	Assessment Objective	What you've written
8-9	**AO1**	• Shows a critical, convincing and well-structured analysis of the poem • Uses well-chosen examples to support interpretation(s)
	AO2	• Gives an insightful analysis of the poet's use of language, structure and form, using technical terms effectively • Presents a detailed exploration of how the poet's techniques affect the reader
6-7	**AO1**	• Presents a thoughtful, well-developed analysis of the poem • Uses a range of examples to support the interpretation(s)
	AO2	• Explores the poet's use of language and/or structure and/or form in detail, using correct technical terms • Examines the effect of the poet's techniques on the reader
4-5	**AO1**	• Gives a clear analysis of the poem • Provides some references and detail related to the interpretation of the poem
	AO2	• Gives some explanation of the poet's use of language and/or structure and/or form, using some relevant technical terms • Explains how some of the techniques used in the poem affect the reader

You can also be awarded grades 1-3. We haven't included any sample answer extracts at 1-3 level though — so those grades aren't in this mark scheme.

Mark Scheme

Now you're a Question 1 expert, here's the mark scheme for Question 2. This question will ask you to write about two poems, but don't fear — this page shows you the sorts of things you'll need to do in your answer.

Use this mark scheme for the answers to Question 2

1) Question 2 will ask you to **compare** two poems.

2) Remember, this question is **only** worth **8 marks**, so you **don't** want to spend **too long** on your answer.

3) This question is all about the **techniques** the poets have used and how they **affect the reader**. Your answer must focus on **similarities** and **differences** between the **language**, **form** and **structure** used in the two poems.

Grade	Assessment Objective	What you've written
8-9	AO2	• Explores similarities and differences between the use of language, structure and form in the two poems, using technical terms effectively • Convincingly explores and compares the ways the poets' techniques affect the reader
6-7	AO2	• Gives a thoughtful comparison of the poets' use of language and/or structure and/or form, using appropriate technical terms • Compares the effects of the poets' techniques on the reader
4-5	AO2	• Compares how the poets have used language and/or structure and/or form, using some relevant technical terms • Compares the way some of the poets' techniques affect the reader

You can also be awarded **grades 1-3**. We **haven't included** any **sample answer extracts** at 1-3 level though — so those grades aren't in this mark scheme.

Look out for quotes and examples in the answer extracts

1) When the examiner marks your answers, he or she will be paying close attention to whether you've used quotes and examples from the poems to back up your arguments.

2) Think like an examiner when you're marking the answer extracts on the next few pages and look out for the way the extracts use evidence from the poems:

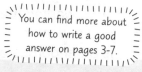 You can find more about how to write a good answer on pages 3-7.

- The quotes and examples should have been carefully chosen — they must be relevant to the point being made.
- There's no need to quote large chunks of text.
- Exact quotes should be inside quotation marks (" ") like this: "The wind howled down the valley."
- If the text has been rephrased, you don't need quotation marks.
  - E.g. The wind is very loud in the valley.
- Wherever possible, quotes should be integrated into the sentences so that the writing flows nicely.
  - E.g. The personification in "The wind howled down the valley" emphasises how loud the wind is.

Listen Mr Oxford Don

John Agard was born in **Guyana**, **South America**, in 1949. He later moved to **Britain** in 1977. He is of **mixed race**, and a lot of his poetry deals with themes such as **identity**, **prejudice** and **stereotypes**.

> Q1   Read the poem below. What do you think the poet is saying about what life can be like for an immigrant in Britain? How does he present these ideas?
>
> **(24 marks)**

Listen Mr Oxford Don

Me not no Oxford don
me a simple immigrant
from Clapham Common
I didn't graduate
5 I immigrate

But listen Mr Oxford don
I'm a man on de run
and a man on de run
is a dangerous one

10 I ent have no gun
I ent have no knife
but mugging de Queen's English
is the story of my life

I don't need no axe
15 to split/ up yu syntax
I don't need no hammer
to mash/ up yu grammar

I warning you Mr Oxford don
I'm a wanted man
20 and a wanted man
is a dangerous one

Dem accuse me of assault
on de Oxford dictionary/
imagine a concise peaceful man like me/
25 dem want me serve time
for inciting rhyme to riot
but I tekking it quiet
down here in Clapham Common

I'm not a violent man Mr Oxford don
30 I only armed wit mih human breath
but human breath
is a dangerous weapon

So mek dem send one big word after me
I ent serving no jail sentence
35 I slashing suffix in self-defence
I bashing future wit present tense
and if necessary

I making de Queen's English accessory/ to my offence

John Agard

Here's a man who
does need an axe.

John Agard

This is your first lot of **sample answer extracts**. For each one, think about where it fits in the **mark scheme** for **Question 1** on **p.34**. Most answers won't fit perfectly into one band, so concentrate on finding the **best fit**.

1

The poet uses non-standard English throughout the poem to replicate the narrator's accent and to show how immigrants can be looked down upon for the way they speak. For example, the narrator says "Me not no Oxford don / me a simple immigrant". The "Oxford don" can be seen to represent British culture and standard English, therefore the use of incorrect grammar in these lines in particular emphasises how the narrator feels judged for not speaking standard English. The narrator then goes on to use language cleverly in the poem to show that people underestimate immigrants. In the lines "I didn't graduate / I immigrate", the narrator leaves the 'd' off 'immigrated' to create a rhyming couplet. This hints at the poet's belief that people shouldn't look down on immigrants for how they speak.

a) Write down the grade band (4-5, 6-7 or 8-9) that you think this answer falls into.

b) Give at least two reasons why you chose that grade.

2

The poet uses violent imagery to show how immigrants can feel unfairly judged and criminalised for the way they speak. The metaphor of the narrator "mugging de Queen's English" is evocative of threat and theft, and by presenting the narrator as an attacker of the monarchy, it suggests that people think their use of the English language is violent. The narrator exaggerates this perception of immigrants by stating "I don't need no axe / to split/ up yu syntax". This uses "yu" to directly address the reader and create a threatening tone, a slash to literally split up the sentence, and the repeated "ax" sound to draw a parallel between weapons and language. By juxtaposing violence and language in this hyperbolic way, the poet creates a sense of irony because using language to express your identity is not a crime.

a) Write down the grade band (4-5, 6-7 or 8-9) that you think this answer falls into.

b) Give at least two reasons why you chose that grade.

3

The poet shows that sometimes British people aren't very understanding of immigrants living in Britain. The narrator describes how some people in Britain think that they are "mugging de Queen's English" because they speak with an accent. Prison language like "serve time" and "jail sentence" shows that people think the way the narrator speaks is wrong and needs to be changed, but the narrator is proud of their culture and thinks that how they speak should be allowed. This is done by using incorrect grammar throughout the poem to reflect the way they speak, such as "I ent have no knife". This choice not to use correct grammar shows that the narrator doesn't care what people think and that they are going to carry on talking the way that they do anyway.

a) Write down the grade band (4-5, 6-7 or 8-9) that you think this answer falls into.

b) Give at least two reasons why you chose that grade.

Neighbours

Benjamin Zephaniah was born in Birmingham in 1958. His parents are from the **Caribbean** and his poetry is influenced by his **Jamaican** heritage. His poems often use **humour** to address serious issues such as **racism**.

> Q2   'Listen Mr Oxford Don' and 'Neighbours' both challenge prejudice.
> Compare the methods the poets use to present ideas about prejudice.
>
> **(8 marks)**

Neighbours

I am the type you are supposed to fear
Black and foreign
Big and dreadlocks
An uneducated grass eater.

5   I talk in tongues
I chant at night
I appear anywhere,
I sleep with lions
And when the moon gets me
10   I am a Wailer.

I am moving in
Next door to you
So you can get to know me,
You will see my shadow
15   In the bathroom window,
My aromas will occupy
Your space,
Our ball will be in your court.
How will you feel?

20   You should feel good
You have been chosen.

I am the type you are supposed to love
Dark and mysterious
Tall and natural
25   Thinking, tea total.
I talk in schools
I sing on TV
I am in the papers,
I keep cool cats

30   And when the sun is shining
I go Carnival.

Benjamin Zephaniah

They do look quite cuddly,
but I wouldn't advise
having a snuggle.

Benjamin Zephaniah

You need to **compare** two poems for Question 2, so in the answers below you're looking for points on the **similarities** and **differences** between the poems. Use the mark scheme on **page 35** to give you a hand...

1

Both poets use the structure of their poems to challenge prejudice. For example, the first stanza of 'Listen Mr Oxford Don' has a calm tone, created by the way the narrator casts themselves as a "simple immigrant" compared to the Oxford don, and how they seem to accept this. However, the tone becomes more forceful in the second stanza when the narrator firmly tells the Oxford don to "listen". This shift in tone is emphasised through the repetition of "a man on de run" and the heavy alliterative 'd' sounds, which show how the narrator changes and challenges the idea of the "simple immigrant". 'Neighbours' is structured differently in that the first two stanzas address the negative opinions that people might have of the narrator. These are then directly reversed in the last two stanzas. For example, "I talk in tongues" becomes "I talk in schools". Structuring the poem in this way allows the poet to directly counter people's prejudices and makes the reader think about challenging their own prejudices.

a)   Write down the grade band (4-5, 6-7 or 8-9) that you think this answer falls into.

b)   Give at least two reasons why you chose that grade.

2

Both poets use contrasting imagery to challenge views that people might have of immigrants. In 'Listen Mr Oxford Don', violent images of a "gun", "knife" and "axe" contrast with more peaceful imagery, such as the narrator "tekking it quiet". This reflects the poet's message that the narrator isn't harming the English language as some people might believe, but that their way of speaking is equally valid. 'Neighbours' also features contrasting imagery to show that people's perceptions of immigrants are false. The threatening image created in the reader's mind by "Black and foreign / Big and dreadlocks" directly contrasts with "Dark and mysterious / Tall and natural". This emphasises the poet's message that the narrator isn't dangerous or threatening as some people may believe.

a)   Write down the grade band (4-5, 6-7 or 8-9) that you think this answer falls into.

b)   Give at least two reasons why you chose that grade.

3

In the poems, both narrators address someone directly to get across their argument about prejudice. Agard's narrator talks to a "Mr Oxford don", who stands for British culture and the people who may be prejudiced against the narrator. The narrator is bold when they tell the Oxford don to "listen" to them. This direct address makes it clear how they are standing up to people who are prejudiced. 'Neighbours' is slightly different in that the narrator talks to the reader instead. They ask "how will you feel?" when they move in next door, which makes the reader think more about their own prejudices. The narrator also says that "you can get to know me", which shows that they are trying to tackle prejudice by bringing people together and encouraging them to get to know each other.

a)   Write down the grade band (4-5, 6-7 or 8-9) that you think this answer falls into.

b)   Give at least two reasons why you chose that grade.

Overlooking the River Stour

Thomas Hardy (1840-1928) is one of England's best known writers. **Nature** features pretty heavily in his poems and novels. This poem was published in **1917** and is about a river in **Dorset** called the **River Stour**.

> Q1 Read the poem below. What do you think the poet is saying about the river? How does he convey this to the reader?
>
> **(24 marks)**

Overlooking the River Stour

The swallows flew in the curves of an eight
Above the river-gleam
In the wet June's last beam:
Like little crossbows animate
5 The swallows flew in the curves of an eight
Above the river-gleam.

Planing up shavings of crystal spray
A moor-hen darted out
From the bank thereabout,
10 And through the stream-shine ripped his way;
Planing up shavings of crystal spray
A moor-hen darted out.

Closed were the kingcups; and the mead
Dripped in monotonous green,
15 Though the day's morning sheen
Had shown it golden and honeybee'd;
Closed were the kingcups; and the mead
Dripped in monotonous green.

And never I turned my head, alack,
20 While these things met my gaze
Through the pane's drop-drenched glaze,
To see the more behind my back...
O never I turned, but let, alack,
These less things hold my gaze!

Thomas Hardy

> Thomas Hardy lived with his first wife, Emma, by the River Stour. Their marriage was often unhappy and they grew apart, but her death in 1912 greatly affected Hardy and inspired his later poetry.

Glossary

kingcups — yellow flowers similar to buttercups
mead — meadow
alack — a word used to show regret or sorrow

I told you to stop looking
at me — weirdo.

Section Three — Marking Sample Answers

Thomas Hardy

Here are three more sample answer extracts. Read through each one and then have a go at grading them. Make sure that you explain what's **wrong** with each answer as well as what's **right**.

1

The form and structure of the poem reflect the narrator's fixation with the river. The repetitive ABBAAB rhyme scheme includes only two rhyming sounds, reflecting how the narrator focuses so much on the river, but not much else. This unwavering focus is also emphasised through the poem's structure, as each of the first three stanzas focuses closely on one aspect of the riverbank; the first on the "swallows", the second on the "moor-hen", and the third on the meadow and its "kingcups". This structure gives the reader the impression that the narrator is fascinated by every feature of the river in turn. Furthermore, the first two lines of each stanza are repeated at the end to form a refrain, highlighting how transfixed the narrator is by the scene. However, Hardy breaks his own conventions in the final stanza. Rather than focusing on individual aspects of the riverbank, the narrator describes them with the term "these things", which strips them of any distinction, and the lack of a refrain suggests that the repetitive focus has ended.

a) Write down the grade band (4-5, 6-7 or 8-9) that you think this answer falls into.

b) Give at least two reasons why you chose that grade.

2

The narrator is shown to be away from the river both physically and emotionally. In the last stanza they use the phrase "the pane's drop-drenched glaze", which suggests that they are stood behind a window watching nature. This tells the reader that the narrator isn't actually that close to the river. Their emotional distance is shown when they repeat the word "monotonous" in the third stanza, as this tells you that they have become bored by nature. The narrator also seems to regret spending so much time looking at the river when they say "alack". By showing this distance, the poet might be trying to say that while nature is beautiful, it isn't everything in life and people should focus on others more.

a) Write down the grade band (4-5, 6-7 or 8-9) that you think this answer falls into.

b) Give at least two reasons why you chose that grade.

3

The poet uses language associated with precious stones to present the beauty of the river. He uses combined words like "river-gleam" and "stream-shine", as well as phrases such as "crystal spray", to emphasise how glistening the river is. The word "crystal" reminds the reader of precious gemstones, and makes the river seem precious to the narrator. However, these images are often juxtaposed with negative ones. For example, the simile of the swallows flying "Like little crossbows animate" compares the birds to weapons, suggesting the beauty of the river may also cause harm. This can be seen in the suggestion that by appreciating the river's beauty, the narrator has ignored the more important things in life.

a) Write down the grade band (4-5, 6-7 or 8-9) that you think this answer falls into.

b) Give at least two reasons why you chose that grade.

Section Three — Marking Sample Answers

Sonnet

Alice Dunbar-Nelson (1875-1935) wrote short stories and poems. She wrote a lot about her experiences as a **mixed-race woman** — an **unusual** combo for a writer at the time. This poem was published in 1922.

> Q2   Both 'Overlooking the River Stour' and 'Sonnet' discuss feelings about nature.
> Compare the methods the poets use to present these feelings.
>
> **(8 marks)**

Sonnet

    I had not thought of violets late,
    The wild, shy kind that spring beneath your feet
    In wistful April days, when lovers mate
    And wander through the fields in raptures sweet.
5   The thought of violets meant florists' shops,
    And bows and pins, and perfumed papers fine;
    And garish lights, and mincing little fops
    And cabarets and soaps, and deadening wines.
    So far from sweet real things my thoughts had strayed,
10   I had forgot wide fields; and clear brown streams;
    The perfect loveliness that God has made,—
    Wild violets shy and Heaven-mounting dreams.
    And now—unwittingly, you've made me dream
    Of violets, and my soul's forgotten gleam.

Alice Dunbar-Nelson

Glossary

raptures — intense happiness
mincing — speaking or walking in an artificially elegant or dainty way
fops — an old term for men who wear very fancy clothes and are too concerned with their appearance
cabarets — theatrical entertainment where performers sing and dance

Alice Dunbar-Nelson

Hopefully you're getting the **hang** of this — English examiners everywhere will be quaking in their boots. Remember, we're back on **Question 2** now, so that means these extracts should be **comparing** two poems.

1

Both poets use language to present nature as beautiful. In Hardy's poem, the narrator uses colours, such as the word "golden", to make nature seem precious. Gold is an expensive metal, so it makes the reader think the poet wants people to treasure nature more. The water is also described as being like a diamond in the phrase "crystal spray". In 'Sonnet', nature is described more simply, e.g. "clear brown streams". Although "brown" is a less striking colour than gold, the narrator describes it as "perfect loveliness", showing that it is still beautiful. This reminds us that nature doesn't need to be showy to be lovely and even simple things can be very attractive.

a)   Write down the grade band (4-5, 6-7 or 8-9) that you think this answer falls into.

b)   Give at least two reasons why you chose that grade.

2

Both poems explore the link between nature and relationships. Hardy's narrator was so focused on nature that they never "turned" their head to see "the more". This something "more" could be a relationship that they neglected due to focusing on nature, and they realised too late that it was precious. For Dunbar-Nelson's narrator, however, their relationship gives them back an appreciation of "sweet real things", suggesting that a happy relationship can enhance someone's enjoyment of nature. Likewise, by describing lovers in a natural setting "in raptures sweet", Dunbar-Nelson hints that nature can also enhance a relationship. The narrators therefore have different attitudes to the link between nature and relationships. Hardy's narrator believes that nature can have a destructive effect on relationships, while Dunbar-Nelson's narrator believes that nature and relationships can enrich one another.

a)   Write down the grade band (4-5, 6-7 or 8-9) that you think this answer falls into.

b)   Give at least two reasons why you chose that grade.

3

The form of each poem reflects how the narrators feel about nature. In Hardy's poem, the repetitive ABBAAB rhyme scheme, and refrains that present nature as precious and idyllic, such as "Planing up shavings of crystal spray", emphasise the narrator's fascination with nature by reflecting how they never looked away or "turned" their "head". However, the irregular line lengths, which vary from 6 to 10 syllables, create a feeling of uncertainty, which may give the reader the impression that this focus is not wholly positive. In contrast, Dunbar-Nelson's poem uses a regular rhyme scheme and most lines are written in iambic pentameter, which creates a feeling of harmony. This is emphasised by the final rhyming couplet, which adds to the sense of the wholeness and contentment that the narrator derives from nature. While 'Sonnet' ends with a sense of fulfilment, the change in form and lack of a refrain in the final stanza of Hardy's poem hints at the narrator's regret that nature meant they neglected other aspects of life.

a)   Write down the grade band (4-5, 6-7 or 8-9) that you think this answer falls into.

b)   Give at least two reasons why you chose that grade.

Beat! Beat! Drums!

Walt Whitman (1819-1892) was an American poet. His poem 'Beat! Beat! Drums!' was published in **1861**, the same year that the **American Civil War** began. That's a handy clue to what the poem is probably **about**.

> Q1 Read the poem below. What is the poet saying about how war affects people's lives? How does he present these ideas?
>
> **(24 marks)**

Beat! Beat! Drums!

Beat! beat! drums! — blow! bugles! blow!
Through the windows — through doors — burst like a ruthless force,
Into the solemn church, and scatter the congregation,
Into the school where the scholar is studying,
5   Leave not the bridegroom quiet — no happiness must he have now with his bride,
Nor the peaceful farmer any peace, ploughing his field or gathering his grain,
So fierce you whirr and pound you drums — so shrill you bugles blow.

Beat! beat! drums! — blow! bugles! blow!
Over the traffic of cities — over the rumble of wheels in the streets;
10   Are beds prepared for sleepers at night in the houses? no sleepers must sleep in those beds,
No bargainers' bargains by day — no brokers or speculators — would they continue?
Would the talkers be talking? would the singer attempt to sing?
Would the lawyer rise in the court to state his case before the judge?
Then rattle quicker, heavier drums — you bugles wilder blow.

15   Beat! beat! drums! — blow! bugles! blow!
Make no parley — stop for no expostulation,
Mind not the timid — mind not the weeper or prayer,
Mind not the old man beseeching the young man,
Let not the child's voice be heard, nor the mother's entreaties,
20   Make even the trestles to shake the dead where they lie awaiting the hearses,
So strong you thump O terrible drums — so loud you bugles blow.

Walt Whitman

Glossary

bugles — musical instruments which are similar to trumpets
brokers — people who arrange sales between a buyer and a seller
speculators — traders who take high risks to try and make large profits
parley — negotiations between opposing sides
expostulation — an expression of strong disagreement with something
trestles — wooden supports

I never asked for any of this.
All I ever wanted was to play
funky tunes in a soul jazz band.

Section Three — Marking Sample Answers

Walt Whitman

Take a look at these sample answer extracts, then try to give them a grade. If you're a bit unsure, flick back to the mark scheme on page 34 which will give you some pointers.

1

> The poet uses onomatopoeia to show that war has an unpleasant effect on people's lives and that they can't escape it. For example, he uses words such as "pound" and "thump" to describe the sound of the drums, which represent war. This allows the reader to clearly hear these sounds in their mind, which shows them how unpleasant they are and how unwelcome war is to the people in the poem. "Beat! beat! drums!" is almost like onomatopoeia because they are short words which sound like drum beats. "blow! bugles! blow!" are longer sounds which are like the blowing of a bugle. The use of these words throughout the poem make it clearer that people cannot escape the effects of war.

a)   Write down the grade band (4-5, 6-7 or 8-9) that you think this answer falls into.

b)   Give at least two reasons why you chose that grade.

2

> The poet uses contrasting language to illustrate the destructive impact of war on people's lives. The long vowel sounds that are created by words such as "school" and "peaceful", which describe the community, are juxtaposed with harsh onomatopoeic verbs such as "shrill" and "whirr". These verbs mimic the noisy bugles and drums, immersing the reader in the harsh sound of war. This juxtaposition creates a stark contrast in tone and highlights how suddenly and brutally people's lives can be affected by war. Furthermore, most of the lines in the poem describe a different person or group, such as the "farmer", "lawyer" or church "congregation". The way the poem is structured presents these descriptions as a type of list, giving the reader the sense that the number of people affected by war is almost unending.

a)   Write down the grade band (4-5, 6-7 or 8-9) that you think this answer falls into.

b)   Give at least two reasons why you chose that grade.

3

> Whitman uses form and structure to present war as a disruptive force that people can't control. The poem is split into three stanzas of 7 lines and each stanza is structured in a similar way. The phrase "Beat! beat! drums! — blow! bugles! blow!" is repeated at the start of each stanza, the main body of each stanza discusses people who are affected by war, and the last line of each stanza finally describes the power of the drums and bugles. The repetition of this structure gives the impression that the effects of war are uncontrollable. The poem also has lines of varying lengths and doesn't have any regular rhyme or rhythm. This repetitive structure mixed with an irregular form gives the poem a sense of both order and disorder, emphasising the chaos that war causes to people's lives.

a)   Write down the grade band (4-5, 6-7 or 8-9) that you think this answer falls into.

b)   Give at least two reasons why you chose that grade.

Songs for the People

Frances Ellen Watkins Harper (1825-1911) fought to abolish **slavery** and increase **women's rights** in the US. Her writing often focused on **change** — like this poem, which argues that poetry can make the world better.

> Q2 'Beat! Beat! Drums!' and 'Songs for the People' both present forceful arguments. Compare the methods the poets use to create this forceful tone.
>
> **(8 marks)**

Songs for the People

Let me make the songs for the people,
    Songs for the old and young;
Songs to stir like a battle-cry
    Wherever they are sung.

5   Not for the clashing of sabres,
    For carnage nor for strife;
But songs to thrill the hearts of men
    With more abundant life.

Let me make the songs for the weary,
10   Amid life's fever and fret,
Till hearts shall relax their tension,
    And careworn brows forget.

Let me sing for little children,
    Before their footsteps stray,
15   Sweet anthems of love and duty,
    To float o'er life's highway.

I would sing for the poor and aged,
    When shadows dim their sight;
Of the bright and restful mansions,
20   Where there shall be no night.

Our world, so worn and weary,
    Needs music, pure and strong,
To hush the jangle and discords
    Of sorrow, pain, and wrong.

25   Music to soothe all its sorrow,
    Till war and crime shall cease;
And the hearts of men grown tender
    Girdle the world with peace.

Glossary

sabres — long curved swords
Girdle — surround

Frances Ellen Watkins Harper

Frances Ellen Watkins Harper

You've spent the last few pages honing your marking skills — here's one last opportunity to show them off. Then you can say "bring on exam day", because you'll know exactly what those examiners are looking for.

1

Both poets use punctuation to add to the forceful tone. In Whitman's poem, the exclamation marks used in phrases such as "Beat! beat! drums!" place emphasis on the monosyllabic words. This makes the words sound short and sharp to the reader, almost like drum beats or bugle blows. Furthermore, the narrator repeatedly uses question marks in phrases like "would the talkers be talking?", which forcefully emphasises how impossible they think it will be for people to carry on with their lives and ignore war. In contrast, 'Songs for the People' uses end-stopping on nearly every line, with a full stop at the end of each stanza. For example, the line "Songs for the old and young;" is end-stopped. This creates a sense of certainty and finality, which makes the narrator's argument seem powerful and unquestionable.

a)   Write down the grade band (4-5, 6-7 or 8-9) that you think this answer falls into.

b)   Give at least two reasons why you chose that grade.

2

Both poets use violent language to create a forceful tone. In 'Beat! Beat! Drums!', war is personified as being able to "burst" into church and "scatter" people; the fact that prayer cannot save people highlights the ruthlessness of war. The plosive 'b' sound in "burst" reinforces the suddenness of the action, suggesting that there is no time for people to react and thus strengthening the idea that war is beyond human control. In 'Songs for the People', Harper compares songs to a "battle-cry" to highlight their power, but the word "Not" before "sabres" and "carnage" negates the suggestion of violence. Placing "Not" at the start of the stanza gives it emphasis, adding force to Harper's message that songs and poems should promote peace. Whereas Harper's poem uses this forceful tone to suggest there is hope for change in the future, the violent language in Whitman's poem escalates until even the "dead" are affected, reminding the reader of the lasting cost of war.

a)   Write down the grade band (4-5, 6-7 or 8-9) that you think this answer falls into.

b)   Give at least two reasons why you chose that grade.

3

Both poets use repetition to create a forceful argument. In 'Beat! Beat! Drums!', the line "Beat! beat! drums! — blow! bugles! blow!" is repeated at the start of each stanza. The noise represents war, and this repetition shows that war cannot be stopped or ignored. The repetition of "mind not" in sentences like "Mind not the timid — mind not the weeper or prayer" shows how terrible war is and how it will affect everyone. In 'Songs for the People', the poet repeats "Let me make the songs", showing how she thinks this is an important way to reach people and make things better. She also uses repetition of "to" in verbs like "to stir" and "to thrill", and these verbs highlight the positive effect that songs and poetry can have.

a)   Write down the grade band (4-5, 6-7 or 8-9) that you think this answer falls into.

b)   Give at least two reasons why you chose that grade.

Time does not bring relief — Edna St. Vincent Millay

Here's your first **sample exam** — hooray.   You'll have **45 minutes** to answer **both questions** in the exam.
Don't forget that you can pick up a **lot more marks** in Question 1, so you'll need to **divide your time** wisely.

> Q1   Read the poem below. What do you think the poet is saying about what it
> is like to remember a loved one? How does the poet convey these ideas?
>
> **(24 marks)**

Time does not bring relief

Time does not bring relief; you all have lied
Who told me time would ease me of my pain!
I miss him in the weeping of the rain;
I want him at the shrinking of the tide;
5   The old snows melt from every mountain-side,
And last year's leaves are smoke in every lane;
But last year's bitter loving must remain
Heaped on my heart, and my old thoughts abide.
There are a hundred places where I fear
10   To go, — so with his memory they brim.
And entering with relief some quiet place
Where never fell his foot or shone his face
I say, "There is no memory of him here!"
And so stand stricken, so remembering him.

Edna St. Vincent Millay

Farewell, Sweet Dust — Elinor Wylie

> Q2 The narrators of 'Time does not bring relief' and 'Farewell, Sweet Dust'
> have different attitudes to the loss of a loved one. Compare the methods
> used by the poets to present these attitudes.
>
> **(8 marks)**

Farewell, Sweet Dust

Now I have lost you, I must scatter
All of you on the air henceforth;
Not that to me it can ever matter
But it's only fair to the rest of the earth.

5   Now especially, when it is winter
And the sun's not half so bright as he was,
Who wouldn't be glad to find a splinter
That once was you, in the frozen grass?

      Snowflakes, too, will be softer feathered,
10   Clouds, perhaps, will be whiter plumed;
Rain, whose brilliance you caught and gathered,
Purer silver have reassumed.

      Farewell, sweet dust; I was never a miser:
Once, for a minute, I made you mine:
15   Now you are gone, I am none the wiser
But the leaves of the willow are bright as wine.

Elinor Wylie

Solitude — Ella Wheeler Wilcox

You've arrived at the final set of practice exam questions, and that means this is your final pair of poems. You know the drill, but don't forget to spend a bit of time annotating before you jot down your essay plans.

> Q1 Read the poem below. What do you think the poet is saying about isolation? How does the poet convey their ideas?
>
> **(24 marks)**

Solitude

Laugh, and the world laughs with you;
Weep, and you weep alone;
For the sad old earth must borrow its mirth,
But has trouble enough of its own.
5   Sing, and the hills will answer;
Sigh, it is lost on the air;
The echoes bound to a joyful sound,
But shrink from voicing care.

Rejoice, and men will seek you;
10 Grieve, and they turn and go;
They want full measure of all your pleasure,
But they do not need your woe.
Be glad, and your friends are many;
Be sad, and you lose them all,
15 There are none to decline your nectared wine,
But alone you must drink life's gall.

Feast, and your halls are crowded;
Fast, and the world goes by.
Succeed and give, and it helps you live,
20 But no man can help you die.
There is room in the halls of pleasure
For a large and lordly train,
But one by one we must all file on
Through the narrow aisles of pain.

Ella Wheeler Wilcox

Glossary

mirth — joy
gall — bitterness

Ode on Solitude — Alexander Pope

Q2 The narrators of 'Solitude' and 'Ode on Solitude' reveal their feelings about being alone. Compare the methods used to present these feelings in the two poems.

(8 marks)

Ode on Solitude

Happy the man, whose wish and care
    A few paternal acres bound,
Content to breathe his native air,
        In his own ground.

5   Whose herds with milk, whose fields with bread,
    Whose flocks supply him with attire,
Whose trees in summer yield him shade,
        In winter fire.

Blest, who can unconcernedly find
10   Hours, days, and years slide soft away,
In health of body, peace of mind,
        Quiet by day,

Sound sleep by night; study and ease
    Together mixed; sweet recreation;
15   And innocence, which most does please,
        With meditation.

Thus let me live, unseen, unknown;
    Thus unlamented let me die;
Steal from the world, and not a stone
20   Tell where I lie.

Alexander Pope

Answers

These are only suggested answers — there are lots of different possible answers to these questions. Just make sure that you back up all your points with evidence from the poems.

Section Two — Unseen Poetry Practice

Page 15 — Tattoos

Warm-up Questions

1) The poem is about someone who remembers looking at their grandmother's tattoos and how they faded as she aged.

2) The grandchild's point of view creates a more objective description of the tattoos and how they changed. It also allows a shift from childlike descriptions of the tattoos to more abstract and mature ones.

3) Admiration for the narrator's grandmother is shown through the colourful and lively imagery used when remembering her tattoos. However, the narrator is more sorrowful in the last 7 lines as they remember her losing her memory and dying. This is reflected by the steady rhythm, which creates a solemn mood.

4) The tattoos represent the grandmother's ageing process — as she aged, the once bright and colourful tattoos of her youth faded to reflect how her body and mind deteriorated.

5) The poet may have used language associated with sailing to reflect the grandmother's life. Initially, the galleon represents a sense of adventure, and is strong and sturdy, reflecting the boldness of the grandmother's youth. However, it later comes "to rest", emphasising the certainty of ageing and death.

6) The word "bravado" suggests the grandmother lived a confident, carefree life in her youth — perhaps to the point of overconfidence.

7) The narrator seems sad at their grandmother's ageing. This is reflected by their melancholy language. For example, they use a metaphor to describe her in old age as a sailing boat with "deflated" sails.

8) The poem consists of one continuous stanza that reflects the grandmother's life. The irregular form in the first half of the poem represents her adventurous, varied youth. Then, after line 17, the shorter lines symbolise her life fading away over time in the same way her tattoos faded.

Focus on... Imagery

1) a) The poet uses a simile describing the tattoos as being "mysterious as runes."

   b) This relates the grandmother's tattoos to magical letters of ancient alphabets, suggesting the narrator found their grandmother intriguing.

2) The metaphor of her memory as shipwrecked implies that her memory was destroyed, as though she suffered from a disease. It also suggests this deterioration was violent and catastrophic

3) The use of the maritime measurement "fathom" reinforces the theme of discovery and sailing. One fathom is equal to six feet, so the poet could be implying that the grandmother has died and been buried 'six feet under'.

Exam-style Question — Part 1

You'll need to spend about 25 minutes on this, and your answer will probably bring in some of the things you thought about when you answered the other questions on the page. Here are some points you could include in your answer:

- The grandmother's tattoos are used as an extended metaphor for her life. As a young woman, her tattoos were colourful and "unblurred by time", suggesting she had a happy and carefree life. However, the narrator describes how the "colours faded", which suggests that she lost her energy and sparkle as she aged.

- The narrator's descriptions of their grandmother's tattoos are very vivid. The description of "each angry thorn on the blue-stemmed rose" shows that the narrator remembers every detail of her tattoos and suggests that they spent a lot of time together.

- The narrator implies that their grandmother was a confident young woman when they state that her tattoos were "bold and clear". By continuing the poem's extended metaphor, the reader gets the sense that the grandmother was as "bold" as the tattoos she had.

- The form of the poem reflects the grandmother's adventurous life. The poem consists of one 23-line stanza, which could symbolise the grandmother's life. The irregular structure reflects how the narrator believes that their grandmother's life wasn't conventional.

- The narrator describes how their grandmother has been affected by ageing. The metaphor "her world shrank to a small island in the brain" uses short, mostly monosyllabic language to show the sadness caused by the grandmother's deterioration. The figurative language also shows that now that the narrator is older, they're more capable of understanding the effects of ageing and memory loss.

- The narrator describes the grandmother's tattoos as mystical. This is shown in the simile "they seemed as mysterious as runes to me". Runes were often believed to possess magical qualities and so in comparing the tattoos to runes, it can be interpreted that the narrator believed their grandmother had a magical aura to her.

Page 17 — The Ageing Schoolmaster

Warm-up Questions

1) In the poem, a schoolmaster is thinking about how he will eventually die. He fondly remembers his youth and has no desire to upset his young pupils by telling them they will die.

2) The second stanza has a resigned mood. This is created as the narrator knows "absolutely" that he will not reacquaint himself with "joy". However, a nostalgic mood is also created when the narrator thinks of when he "rolled, a gormless boy", as it suggests he had fun in his youth.

3) While the use of words such as "rollicked" presents the narrator's childhood as carefree, he also states that he feels "no pinch or prick of envy" when he sees his younger pupils. This implies that although he enjoyed his childhood, he doesn't long to return to it.

4) The phrase "I sniff the smell of ink and chalk and my mortality" appeals to the sense of smell. It shows how mortality

Answers

has pervaded the classroom, suggesting the narrator strongly links the two and that mortality is ever present in his mind.

5) The "april faces / That gleam" before the narrator "like apples ranged on shelves" is a simile. It compares the pupils to shiny apples. The way they "gleam" presents them as keen and optimistic in contrast to the narrator. The fact that the pupils are compared to fresh fruit emphasises the idea that they are young and much further away from death than the narrator.

6) a) The poet presents both the narrator in his youth and the young pupils as being optimistic and blissfully unaware of their own mortality.

b) Getting older is presented as a process that is out of the narrator's control. He wonders "when precisely tolled the bell" that brought him into adulthood and was "summoned" from his childhood, which suggests that time has control over him.

c) The poet presents death as a "huge inevitability", meaning it is a certainty that weighs down heavily on the narrator. Because death preoccupies the thoughts of the only adult in the poem, the poet could be implying that death only becomes an issue when you age and lose your sense of youthful naivety.

7) The poet uses a regular ABCB rhyme scheme. This gives the poem a flowing rhythm, which could reflect the schoolmaster's nostalgic mood as he reflects on his memories and the future. The regular rhyme scheme also adds to the sense that ageing is inevitable and that life seems monotonous to the narrator as he grows older.

8) The image of "death, who carries off all the prizes" is an example of personification. It presents death as a victor in a competition, which makes death seem more real and present to the reader.

Focus on... Vocabulary

1) Autumn "finds" the narrator, which suggests that the narrator has a passive role compared to the passing of time, which controls him. The narrator almost seems to be accepting of this.

2) He could either be referring to the classroom or to the narrator's life as an older adult, as "chill" and "autumnal" are associated with the later half of the year.

3) The poet uses the semantic field of seasons (summer and autumn) to reflect different parts of the human life span. This emphasises that ageing is a natural process, even if it is not entirely welcome. The "summer liberties" are presented as being the points in life when you are happiest and freest, as shown when the narrator "rollicked round the playground". Autumn is symbolic of the narrator's adult years — autumn is the season when plants begin to die, which reflects the narrator growing older.

Exam-style Question — Part 2

You'll need to spend about 15 minutes on this, and your answer will probably bring in some of the things you thought about when you answered the other questions on the two poems. These are some points you could mention:

- One major difference in the methods used to present attitudes towards ageing is that 'Tattoos' is from the perspective of someone witnessing the ageing of a loved one, whereas 'The Ageing Schoolmaster' is from the perspective of someone who themselves is ageing.

- Both poems compare the aged person to their youthful self. In 'Tattoos', the narrator imagines their grandmother "in her youth" before recounting how her "memory was shipwrecked". Similarly, in 'The Ageing Schoolmaster', the narrator remembers how he "rolled, a gormless boy". These contrasts emphasise each figure's ageing.

- Both poems use sensory language to convey attitudes towards getting older. The narrator of Patten's poem focuses heavily on the sense of sight. They remember the "unblurred" tattoos and the bold "colours", but also how the tattoos faded. This helps the reader to visualise the effects of ageing on the grandmother. In 'The Ageing Schoolmaster', the narrator uses multiple senses, such as smell ("sniff"), touch ("prick") and sound ("tolled"), which suggests the notion of death not only plagues his thoughts, but has taken over his senses too.

- Both narrators use alliteration when describing the effects of ageing. In 'Tattoos', the narrator describes how no "burst blood vessels sullied / the breast of the blue-bird" in the grandmother's youth. The repeated 'b' sound almost recreates the sound of the vessels bursting, emphasising the grandmother's physical deterioration as she aged. In 'The Ageing Schoolmaster', the narrator describes how he "rolled" and "rollicked round the playground" when he was a child. This phrase uses alliteration of the 'r' sound to create a lively, upbeat rhythm, which presents his youth as jovial and carefree.

Page 19 — Originally

Warm-up Questions

1) The poem is about a child who remembers when she and her family emigrated to another country, and the difficulties they faced during and after moving.

2) The repetition is almost like a chant, which creates the sense that her brothers are desperate to go back home. The repetition covers two lines, which creates a visual separation between the two words and reflects the distance the boys feel from their home.

3) This metaphor compares growing up to moving away. It highlights how getting older is always a big change, that this change is universal in that everyone goes through it, and that the changes are constant throughout childhood.

4) The end-stopping emphasises how short the sentence is. This mimics the suddenness it describes.

5) This shows that although the narrator is starting to fit into her new country, she has retained her Scottish dialect. This emphasises how important her cultural identity is to her.

6) The simile "my tongue / shedding its skin like a snake" compares the narrator losing her accent to a snake shedding its skin. The sibilance mimics the sound of a snake hissing, emphasising the image and suggesting that the narrator's change is a natural (although arguably horrifying) process.

7) The use of direct speech, such as *"Where do you come from?",*

Answers

directly involves the reader, making them feel immersed in what the narrator feels as well as encouraging them to question their own roots and experiences.

8) The poem lacks a fixed rhyme scheme, which reflects the narrator's insecurities and lack of control in her unfamiliar new home. However, lines 22 and 23 contain the internal rhyme "space" and "place", which could suggest the narrator is getting used to her new home.

9) The narrator is unsure about her identity, as shown through the final word "hesitate". Along with the question *Originally?*, this suggests that the idea of which place she identifies with the most has been blurred and she may be considering that her new home now forms part of her identity.

Focus on... Mood

1) a) The mood in the first stanza is generally anxious and fearful.

b) The use of the phrase "fell through the fields" emphasises the narrator's lack of control, which creates an uneasy mood. Describing how she is "holding" the "paw" of a toy suggests that she is scared and needs emotional comfort, which adds to the tense, fearful mood of the stanza.

2) The poet uses aspects of form to create a feeling of confusion. The second stanza has a mix of long and short sentences, enjambment, end-stopping and caesurae, which create an irregular rhythm that reflects the narrator's feeling of uncertainty and confusion.

3) a) The questions in the third stanza create a mood of uncertainty.

b) The questions show the narrator doubting her own identity. This is shown by the fact she first questions what she's "lost", followed by questions from other people about her identity. The fact that she hesitates to answer these questions shows her uncertainty.

Exam-style Question — Part 1

You'll need to spend about 25 minutes on this, and your answer will probably bring in some of the things you thought about when you answered the other questions on the page. Here are some points you could include in your answer:

- The narrator presents moving to a new place as being an uncertain experience. This is shown when she holds the "paw" of a "blind toy", as it suggests that she seeks comfort and feels alone when moving. The toy being "blind" emphasises her uncertainty about the journey.

- The narrator presents moving to a new place as an unnatural process. It causes her "parents' anxiety" to stir in her head "like a loose tooth". This simile evokes pain and discomfort, and shows that the parents' anxiety permeates through to her. This simile may relate to the idea that your teeth falling out in your dreams is a sign of underlying worry.

- The narrator shows how moving to a new place can be confusing. The image of "big boys / eating worms" creates a strong sense of her confusion and isolation. The intimidating "big boys" and the strange way they are "eating worms" makes the new place seem completely alien to her. Because she can't "understand" the locals in the new place, she is presented as isolated and different.

- The narrator begins the poem with "We", but transitions to "I" later in the poem. This reinforces her sense of isolation as it suggests she has been forced to become more independent in her new home. This also relates to the metaphor "All childhood is an emigration", which compares growing up to moving away — the narrator has both moved home and grown up, which is why she has had to become more independent.

- The poem's form reflects the narrator's feelings at moving away. It lacks a fixed rhyme scheme and has varying rhythms, which reflect her sense of insecurity in her new home. However, the poem's three 8-line stanzas create some regularity, hinting at her conflicted feelings about identity in her new home.

- The narrator realises that she has to adapt in a new place. The simile "my tongue / shedding its skin like a snake" suggests she passively lost her old language, as snakes shed skin naturally. The sibilance creates a soft sound, which emphasises how easily she adopted the new language, despite being quite resilient when

she first declared "I want our own country".

Page 21 — Hard Water

Warm-up Questions

1) The poem is about a narrator who remembers a holiday to Wales and how they experienced the soft water there. The poem then shifts to the narrator describing their hometown and appreciating both the hard water and the people.

2) The poem is written in free verse, which reflects the "straight talk" of the narrator's hometown. With its irregular metre, the form also reflects the "not quite clean" characteristic of hard water.

3) The tone becomes simpler and more appreciative in the second stanza, which is shown in line 4: "but I loved coming home to this". The word "but" reflects the "straight talk" and introduces the matter-of-fact tone.

4) The monosyllabic, one-word sentences used to describe the hard water reflect the flat pronunciation and vowels of the local accent, and so create a connection between the water and the local people.

5) The poet uses an extended metaphor to compare the hard water to the narrator's hometown and its residents.

6) The phrase "sour steam" is an example of sibilance. The repeated 's' sound mirrors the hissing of the cooling towers, immersing the reader in the brewery town setting.

7) The "different cleverness" refers to the local, hardworking community. Although the narrator has had "book-learning", they believe that the "early mornings" of hard work are still a type of cleverness.

8) The narrator states that they "loved coming home" to the hard water to highlight their sense of pride in it. As the poem uses this hard water as an extended metaphor for their hometown, it can be seen that the narrator shares the same sense of pride for their hometown.

9) The poem's final line is shorter than the others, with only three words. This places emphasis on it, leaving the reader with a strong final impression of the narrator's sense of "belonging" in their hometown.

Answers

Focus on... Voice

1) The first-person narrator gives the reader a personal insight into hard water and the narrator's connection with it. It also stresses the personal connection between the hard water and the narrator's local community.

2) a) *"don't get mardy"*

b) The dialect is used in brief, colloquial examples of direct speech, giving the reader a better sense of what the local speech sounds like. By using dialect words, the blunt and straight-talking nature of the locals is emphasised, further reinforcing the poem's extended metaphor.

Exam-style Question — Part 2

You'll need to spend about 15 minutes on this, and your answer will probably bring in some of the things you thought about when you answered the other questions on the two poems. These are some points you could mention:

- Both narrators associate their roots with a physical location. In 'Originally', the narrator states *"I want our own country"*, which uses the possessive determiner *"our"* to imply that she feels a sense of ownership over it. In 'Hard Water', the narrator "loved coming home", despite trying the "soft stuff" in Wales. This shows how they are glad to be coming back to their hometown and its hard water. Both narrators express a fondness for their roots.

- The narrator of 'Originally' moves away from their roots, whereas the narrator of 'Hard Water' has returned to theirs. Duffy's narrator describes how "the miles rushed back to the city", which personifies "miles" and uses the onomatopoeic verb "rushed" to create the sense that she is moving away from her roots quickly. The narrator of 'Hard Water' is presented as "coming home", which suggests a warm and close connection to their roots.

- Both narrators show a fondness for their linguistic roots. In Duffy's poem, the phrase a "skelf of shame" shows how the narrator has retained her Scottish dialect in her new country, suggesting it's an integral part of her identity. However, her tongue sheds "its skin like a snake", implying that her identity is undergoing change. In 'Hard Water',

the narrator describes the "straight talk", showing an appreciation of the local accent, particularly how "Flat" and "Straight" it is. The narrator uses direct speech such as *"don't get mardy"* to give the reader a better understanding of what the dialect sounds like.

- Both poems are written in free verse, which reflects each narrator's feelings towards their roots. The lack of a rhyme scheme in 'Originally' creates a sense of irregularity, which highlights how insecure moving away from her roots makes her feel. However, the internal rhyme of "space" and "place" in lines 22-23 hint that she is becoming less insecure. 'Hard Water' is also written in free verse. This reflects the "straight talk" and therefore emphasises how the narrator appreciates the "blunt" local dialect. The free verse form in 'Originally' suggests unfamiliarity and uncertainty, whereas in 'Hard Water' it hints at an attachment to the locals.

Page 23 — Island Man

Warm-up Questions

1) The poem is about a man waking up after dreaming of his previous home on a Caribbean island, before gradually coming back to the reality of his life in London.

2) Referring to the man in the poem as "island man" emphasises his close connection to where he came from. It also suggests he feels separated from London, by emphasising that he is from a different place. Referring to him as an "island" might also make him seem emotionally cut-off to the reader, suggesting he may be lonely.

3) The lines show how important the sights and sounds of the Caribbean are to him, as they are in his thoughts and dreams at the point where he is starting to wake up. The fact that they are in his mind suggests a feeling of longing for his Caribbean island.

4) The repetition of the words creates a sense of confusion which might reflect the man's sleepiness as he wakes up. It also echoes the rocking sound of the tides that the man remembers on the island, helping the reader to imagine the experience of being on the island.

5) Words like "roar" and "surge" are used to describe the London traffic that the man can hear while he wakes. These words could also be used to describe the movement of the tide, suggesting that the man is imagining that he is actually near the Caribbean sea. The use of this language shows both that the man is disoriented or still dreaming, and also how strong his memories of the Caribbean are, as they influence the way he experiences London.

6) The phrase "fishermen pushing out to sea / the sun surfacing defiantly" uses sibilance. The soft 's' and 'sh' sounds echo the sounds of the sea, helping the reader to imagine being on the man's island. The sibilance also has a soothing effect, suggesting how much calmer and more relaxing the island was compared to London.

7) a) Bright colours are used in the description of the man's Caribbean island ("blue surf" and "emerald island"), while the only colour used to describe London is "grey".

b) The use of contrasting colours to describe the island and London makes the man's previous home seem like a beautiful paradise, while London seems dreary and drab.

8) The final line, "Another London day", suggests that the man wakes up this way every morning and makes his life in London seem repetitive and boring. The line is separated from the rest of the poem, which reflects the fact that he has come out of his dream and must now face the reality of his day.

Focus on... Form

1) The line is very short, which makes the start of the poem abrupt, as if the man has woken up suddenly. It also helps to set the scene of the poem, giving the reader a sense of the time of day.

2) Enjambment makes the poem seem disordered rather than carefully controlled. This reflects the man's sleepiness as he wakes up, showing that he is disoriented and isn't fully aware of his surroundings yet.

3) The increased spacing before "groggily groggily" emphasises these words to the reader, and therefore how disorientated the man feels as he begins to wake up. The way the

phrase "to surge of wheels" is set far off to the right of the line also draws attention to this phrase and reflects how the jarring sounds of traffic interrupt the man's dreams, just as the layout interrupts the flow of the poem.

Exam-style Question — Part 1

You'll need to spend about 25 minutes on this, and your answer will probably bring in some of the things you thought about when you answered the other questions on the page. Here are some points you could include in your answer:

- The narrator uses contrasts between nature and machinery to emphasise the different lifestyles in the Caribbean and London. When describing the Caribbean, the narrator uses a semantic field of nature, such as the "surf" and the "emerald island". This makes the Caribbean seem like a natural paradise. Although the semantic field of nature continues in the descriptions of London, it is combined with imagery of machinery, such as the "grey metallic soar" and a "surge of wheels". This creates the impression that it is a less 'natural' place than the Caribbean.

- Nichols uses contrasting sounds to make the Caribbean seem more appealing than London. In the Caribbean, the sound of "steady breaking" creates an image of soft waves crashing on the shore. The sibilance in "sun surfacing" is soothing, which reinforces the gentle atmosphere in the Caribbean. This contrasts with the onomatopoeic "roar" of London, which is loud and brash, and makes London seem harsh and unfriendly.

- Life in London seems monotonous compared to life in the Caribbean. The fact the man "heaves" himself out of bed suggests that getting up is a chore, which could imply that he finds life in London dull. This is emphasised by the final line "Another London day". The word "Another" at the start of the line emphasises the fact that the man wakes up this way every morning, making his routine seem repetitive. In contrast, life in the Caribbean seems exciting, as it is associated with active verbs. Instead of heaving themselves out of bed, the fishermen are "pushing out to sea"; this image creates a sense of adventure.

- The poem's form makes life in London seem unnatural. The form becomes more irregular as it moves from describing the Caribbean to London. While the poem starts with the lines aligned to the left, the form changes at the poem's volta with the words "groggily groggily". Here, the form becomes fragmented, with the lines positioned unusually on the right of the page as the poem describes London. This makes life in London seem strange and unnatural.

- The Caribbean is described using more comforting language than London. For example, the verb "wombing" is associated with motherhood, which makes the Caribbean seem like a safe, cosy place. London, however, is a harsh, noisy place where the narrator can't relax: he is forced to get up.

Page 25 — Remember

Warm-up Questions

1) The poem is about the importance of remembering where we come from and the world around us — it describes several things the reader should "Remember", including their links to family and nature.

2) The phrase "Remember the sky that you were born under" encourages the reader to remember the place where they were born, while "know each of the star's stories" suggests they should be aware of their place in the universe. Both images emphasise to the reader the importance of nature in understanding the world.

3) Using the second person allows the narrator to develop a closer connection with the reader and encourages them to think about the ideas in the poem and how they relate to their own life.

4) Presenting the poem as one continuous stanza makes the different ideas in the poem flow into one another — this shows how all of the things to remember from "Remember the sky that you were born under" to "Remember the dance language is, that life is" are of equal importance to the narrator.

5) Enjambment is used in the sentence "She knows the / origin of this universe." This places emphasis on the word "origin", showing how important the narrator thinks

it is to be aware of the past and where you have come from.

6) The poet personifies the wind by saying "Remember the wind. Remember her voice. She knows the / origin of this universe." The wind is described as having a voice and a deep understanding of the universe. This stresses how important the narrator believes nature is, as it helps people to feel more connected to the universe.

7) A metaphor is used in the phrase "you are all people and all people / are you." This stresses how every individual is connected to everyone else. Describing this idea in two different ways, moving from "you" to "all people" and then back to "you", emphasises this message by reinforcing the link between the reader and the rest of society.

8) The overall mood of the poem is thoughtful and contemplative. This is created by the continuous appeals to the reader to "Remember", which suggest that the reader should pause and take the time to really think about the world around them and their heritage. The frequent references to nature also help to create a calm tone in the poem.

Focus on... Repetition

1) Repeating the imperative "Remember" as a command throughout the poem puts across a sense of urgency to the reader about not forgetting their place in the world. The repetition also mimics the action of remembering, emphasising to the reader the importance of constantly remembering and being aware of the world around them.

2) a) The poet uses repetition of "her" and "hers" in the phrase "You are evidence of / her life, and her mother's, and hers."

b) This encourages the reader to think about the continuous line of women who have contributed to their life. This emphasises the importance of family and ancestry in understanding how we come to be who we are.

Exam-style Question — Part 2

You'll need to spend about 15 minutes on this, and your answer will probably bring in some of the things you thought about when you answered the other questions

Answers

on the two poems. These are some points you could mention:

- 'Island Man' presents a personal memory by using the third person to describe the experience of one individual. The description of the man as "island man" emphasises how the poem is about this one person and his memories of his original home. 'Remember', on the other hand, presents memory as more universal and part of a broader cultural heritage. The main way this is achieved is through the use of second-person address in sentences like "Remember you are this universe and this / universe is you." By addressing the reader in general, the poet emphasises how certain kinds of memory are shared by everyone, and encourages the reader to remember their links to all people and to all of nature.

- Both poems make use of rhyme and rhythm to present ideas about memory. 'Island Man' has no rhyme scheme, fixed rhythm or stanza length, and uses frequent enjambment, which all help to create a sense of the dreaminess and incoherence experienced by the man as he wakes up "groggily" and remembers where he really is. This suggests that the man's memories are overpowering for him. 'Remember' features a similar lack of rhyme scheme and several long, enjambed lines, which create a sense of flow in the poem. This suggests that remembering the things in the poem — your culture and your place in the world — should be natural and easy.

- Both poems use language related to place and landscape to emphasise the links between memory and identity. 'Island Man' refers to "his small emerald island" which the man returns to in his mind. The possessive "his" shows the sense of belonging he feels towards the island — even though he is now in London, he still feels a close personal connection to the place. This shows how important the memory of the island is to him. Similarly, the narrator of 'Remember' says "Remember the earth whose skin you are". This metaphor shows the close relationship between a person's identity and their environment. It emphasises how important remembering nature is, because humans are part of nature.

- Both poets use repetition to explore memory, but in different ways. 'Island Man' uses repetition to convey the effects of memory. In the poem, the words "comes back" are repeated as the man wakes up to the reality of his life in London. The repetition suggests returning to his normal life from his memory is a struggle, showing the powerful effect of his memories on him. 'Remember' uses repetition to emphasise the poet's main message. Anaphora is used to repeat the word "Remember" throughout the poem. This insistently emphasises to the reader the importance of considering their heritage and their place in the world, and consciously remembering these things.

Page 27 — Crossing the Bar

1) The poem is about someone who is standing by the sea. They are called as if they are being summoned by death. They hope that the journey will be peaceful and that no one will mourn them when they die.

2) Sunset marks the end of the day and approach of sleep. It could therefore symbolise the nearing end of the narrator's life.

3) a) The poet uses personification, as the sandbar is described as "moaning", which is a human action.

   b) The personification of the bar "moaning" gives the impression that it could feel pain at the narrator's passing, but hoping that there will be "no moaning" suggests that the narrator wants the journey to be easy and painless, and doesn't want the world to mourn them.

4) Yes, 'crossing the bar' is an effective extended metaphor for death. It successfully compares the uncertainty of what lies beyond the sandbar with the uncertainty some people feel towards death and the afterlife.

5) The repetition of "When" across stanzas reflects the narrator's feeling of certainty towards crossing the bar and the afterlife. It suggests that they will definitely get there as although they have yet to cross the bar, they realise they will do one day.

6) The verb "hope" creates a tone of uncertainty, as it suggests the narrator isn't sure what will happen when they die. However, it also suggests the narrator is optimistic about the afterlife, despite not knowing exactly what will happen.

7) The narrator is most likely referring to God. A pilot is in control of a person's journey and would navigate a boat through difficult waters, which symbolises God ensuring the narrator's safe passage to Heaven.

8) The poem can be seen as a religious poem in the sense that the narrator is presented as believing in God on multiple occasions. For example, "Pilot" is unusually capitalised, which hints that the narrator may see the "Pilot" as God (a figure whose name is always capitalised). Also, the metaphor of 'crossing the bar' evokes both the action of making the sign of the cross on your chest, as though the narrator is performing a final prayer before they die, and the idea of crossing from this world into the next — the afterlife.

Focus on... Rhyme and Rhythm

1) a) The poem has an ABAB rhyme scheme.

   b) The strict, repetitive nature of this reflects the ebb and flow of the sea. Furthermore, the second and last lines in the final stanza return to the rhyme of the first and third line in the first stanza, which hints at the continuation of life after death.

2) a) The poem has an irregular rhythm due to its inconsistent metre, which varies between lines.

   b) This varying metre and rhythm evokes the ebb and flow of the tide, giving the poem an overall calm and serene mood.

Exam-style Question — Part 1

You'll need to spend about 25 minutes on this, and your answer will probably bring in some of the things you thought about when you answered the other questions on the page. Here are some points you could include in your answer:

- The poem presents the narrator as being accepting and unafraid of death, which is an attitude reflected in the simple phrase "When I have crossed the bar". The monosyllabic language creates a sense of calm.

- The poet uses the extended metaphor of crossing a sandbar to present the narrator's "hope" that they will

Answers

have an easy passage towards death. The narrator wishes that there be "no moaning of the bar" when they cross. This personifies the sandbar, and by hoping that it doesn't make any noises associated with pain, the narrator implies that they want the journey to be a comfortable one.

- The poem suggests that the narrator does not wish to be mourned after their death. This is shown through the phrase "may there be no sadness of farewell, / When I embark", which reinforces the idea that the narrator has accepted death and wants others to know this. The active phrase "I embark" implies that the narrator is choosing to go on the journey and isn't being forced, which suggests they are accepting of their death.

- The narrator's belief in God seems to give them a feeling of solace when facing death. They state "I hope to see my Pilot face to face". The capitalisation of "Pilot" strongly implies that they are referring to God, who is presented as a ship's captain. This suggests God will lead the narrator safely to the afterlife.

- The narrator's acceptance of death is stressed through the poem's gentle rhythm. The lines consist of either 10, 6 or 4 syllables and are mostly in iambic metre. This could reflect the tide ebbing and flowing, and creates a tranquil mood that reflects the narrator's peace of mind. The regular ABAB rhyme scheme further emphasises how the narrator is calm.

- Although accepting and unafraid of death, the narrator sometimes experiences moments of uncertainty towards their fate. This is shown through the use of the word "hope", which implies a sense of doubt, as if the narrator isn't confident that they will make it to the afterlife.

Page 29 — Because I could not stop for Death

Warm-up Questions

1) The narrator is taking a carriage trip with a personification of death. On the trip, the narrator suggests they pass her childhood school before reaching a "House" that symbolises her grave. In the final stanza, the reader learns that the narrator has been dead for centuries.

2) The carriage ride can be seen as an extended metaphor for the narrator's transition from life to death. It is effective as it presents the process of death as a journey — in this case, a journey through the stages of life. A reader may also interpret the carriage ride as the narrator being in a hearse on the way to her funeral.

3) The transition from first-person singular to first-person plural can be seen to mark the start of the narrator's transition from life to death. It's as though she is becoming one with death.

4) "We passed" is repeated at the start of lines 9, 11 and 12. This anaphora creates a sense of forward motion that reflects the carriage journey and emphasises how the narrator passes through various stages of her life.

5) The tone becomes cold and uncomfortable through words such as "quivering" and "Chill", as well as the narrator's realisation that her clothing is not suitable to keep her warm. This makes the reader feel uncomfortable, as it creates the sense that not everything is as pleasant as it first seemed.

6) The unnatural image of the house as "A Swelling of the Ground" presents it as a pile of disturbed earth. The "Swelling" could therefore be the narrator's freshly dug grave and suggests that this grave has now become her home.

7) Death is presented as a gentlemanly figure because he "kindly stopped" for the narrator and also has "Civility". Personifications of death are often evil (e.g. the grim reaper) and are shown as wishing to steal away a person's life, so to have death pick up the narrator and take her to the afterlife without haste seems unusual.

8) The poem is written almost entirely in iambic metre, which mirrors the rhythm of the horses gently pulling the carriage along. The consistency of the metre throughout the poem reflects the certainty of death and the steady progress the narrator makes towards "Eternity".

9) In the first stanza, the narrator calmly states that "Immortality" is in the carriage with them, suggesting that she is aware she is going to the afterlife. In the last stanza, she describes the carriage ride as heading "toward Eternity", which

suggests she believes in an afterlife and is perhaps already there as she narrates.

Focus on... Punctuation

1) The frequently appearing dashes create pauses that slow the pace of the poem. This reflects the leisurely pace of the carriage ride.

2) The full stop here could represent her life coming to an end as the sentence ends. This is reinforced by the fact that the next sentence at the start of the second stanza begins describing the journey, representing that her life has come to an end, and now she is journeying to death.

3) The enjambment in the final stanza increases the pace of the poem. This reflects the narrator's assertion that the "Centuries" which have passed feel "shorter than the Day" she died.

Exam-style Question — Part 2

You'll need to spend about 15 minutes on this, and your answer will probably bring in some of the things you thought about when you answered the other questions on the two poems. These are some points you could mention:

- The narrators of both poems don't show fear towards death. In 'Crossing the Bar', the narrator implies that they welcome death when they "hope" to meet their "Pilot face to face". In 'Because I could not stop for Death', the narrator calmly asserts that 'Death' "kindly stopped" for her, which suggests that she is glad that he did.

- In both poems, death is presented as a relatively pleasant experience. In 'Crossing the Bar', the narrator describes how the tide "Turns again home", which may reveal that they see death as a form of homecoming. In Dickinson's poem, 'Death' has "Civility", which presents him as a courteous gentleman. This gives the reader the impression that the narrator's meeting with 'Death' is almost pleasantly romantic.

- Both poems present their narrator's attitudes through a physical journey. Tennyson uses imagery related to the sea to show the narrator's acceptance of death. The sibilance in "such a tide as moving seems asleep" evokes the narrator being pulled towards the afterlife peacefully by the tide. In Dickinson's poem, the carriage ride symbolises the narrator's passage toward death. Her attitude is presented as calm through the leisurely pace of the carriage ride which travels towards eternity without "haste".

- Both narrators present death as being a passive experience. This is shown in 'Crossing the Bar' when the narrator states "The flood may bear me far". The phrase "may bear" indicates that the narrator has no control over whether the flood will carry them far enough to get to the afterlife. The narrator's passivity is exaggerated through the word "flood", as the huge quantities of water almost make the narrator seem insignificant. The narrator of Dickinson's poem is similarly passive, as shown in the phrase "Because I could not stop for Death". 'Death' is presented as having the active role as he determines the speed of her passage into the afterlife. The narrator is merely a passenger on the journey.

Page 31 — My Father on His Shield

Warm-up Questions

1) The poem is about a narrator who remembers sledding with their father as a child. They remember how their father went off to war and become upset over the fact that they can't bring him back.

2) The sentence establishes how the narrator feels dejected at the loss of their father and how they can't bring him back. This is emphasised as the sentence is short and the words are monosyllabic. This creates a contrast with the rest of the poem, in which enjambment and figurative language are used often. This relative simplicity creates a raw and honest feeling.

3) The poem has no rhyme scheme. This creates a serious tone, as it suggests that the narrator's life has become unbalanced by the loss of the father. The use of enjambment also gives the poem a thoughtful and melancholy mood, as it creates the sense that the narrator is letting their emotions flow out naturally.

4) By placing the flag on the "mantel", it suggests that the family have created a memorial to the father and shows how the war has affected the family's home life. A

mantelpiece is often the centrepiece of a family's living room, which suggests the father was central to their lives. The fact the flag is "folded tight" shows that the family has a great amount of respect for the fallen father, as it suggests that they look after it with care.

5) The father is presented as a strong, rugged figure through the use of the plosive, onomatopoeic verb "pounded", as it emphasises the forcefulness with which he strikes the metal. However, he is also presented as loving and protective when he wraps the "rope in his fist / around" the narrator's "chest".

6) The phrase "steam billowing like a smoke screen" is an example of a simile. This simile uses the military term "smoke screen" to reflect the father's military life. It also foreshadows that the father won't return — smoke screens are used in the military as a tactic to hide things and so it creates an image of the father disappearing.

7) The caesura in the middle of line 18 creates a volta. This signifies the sudden jump from the narrator's happy memory of spending time with their father, to the unhappy memory of their father going away to war on the "troop train".

8) There is a mood of underlying tension in the final two stanzas. This is created through the strong plosive sounds in phrases such as "pounding to beat the iron" and "can't bring him back", as they mimic the sound of the narrator repeatedly and helplessly striking the metal as they realise that they won't get their father back.

9) The fact that the father's shield is only mentioned in the title and not in the main body of the poem perhaps reflects how the father is no longer physically with his family, but is separate from them.

Focus on... Appeals to the Senses

1) a) The poet uses imagery related to touch when describing the rope the father grips "around my chest".

b) It suggests the narrator's memories of their father are vivid and tangible, hinting that they relive them often because they are precious.

2) a) The phrase "pines whishing by" uses onomatopoeia, so it

appeals to the sense of hearing.

b) The word "whishing" imitates the sound of the air rushing past and stresses the speed they're sledding at. This immerses the reader in the experience and makes it sound more exhilarating to show that the narrator enjoyed spending time with their father.

3) The extensive use of sensory language is effective in creating the impression that the narrator has very vivid memories of their father, showing how much they cherish both him and the memories. Sensory language also draws in the reader, allowing them to imagine the feel, sound and sight of the memories.

Exam-style Question — Part 1

You'll need to spend about 25 minutes on this, and your answer will probably bring in some of the things you thought about when you answered the other questions on the page. Here are some points you could include in your answer:

- The narrator is presented as feeling melancholy at the loss of their father. Their sadness is expressed through the phrase "I can't bring him back", as it gives the narrator a resigned quality. The use of the present tense in "can't" suggests that their sadness is ongoing.

- The narrator's positive memories heighten this sense of melancholy. This is shown in the descriptions of sledding, such as "pines whishing by, ice in my eyes, blinking / and squealing". The onomatopoeic verbs "whishing" and "squealing" show how vivid the narrator's memories with their father are. However, "squealing" also has negative connotations and hints at the narrator crying uncontrollably over their lost father.

- The narrator's first-person perspective heightens their feeling of suffering to the reader. Through words such as "I" and "my", the poet shows how personal the suffering is, and by using the first person, the reader feels as if the narrator is talking to them, inviting them to share in their emotional state.

- The poem's form reflects the narrator's feelings over the loss of their father. It is written in free verse, has no fixed rhythm or rhyme scheme, and has uneven line lengths, which all reflect how the narrator doesn't feel complete or settled without their father. It suggests that the father may have brought orderliness or routine to the child's upbringing.

- The military imagery used in the poem reflects the narrator's suffering. The simile of the troop train steam "billowing like a smoke screen" evokes the idea of the narrator losing their father in the smoke. By using military terminology, the poet could be foreshadowing how the father dies in war.

- Sensory language heightens the narrator's sense of bitterness. This is shown in the phrase "pounding to beat the iron flat", where the plosive 'p' and 'b' sounds reflect the force with which the narrator beats the iron and mimic the sound of them hitting the sled. The 'b' sound is repeated throughout the final two stanzas, meaning the sound continues as though the narrator keeps hitting the sled.

Page 33 — Those Winter Sundays

Warm-up Questions

1) In the poem, the narrator remembers their childhood and how their father would wake up early to light the fires in the house. The narrator considers all the sacrifices their father made for their family, and feels guilty for not fully appreciating him or communicating their love for him.

2) The father wakes up early despite it being "blueblack cold". The forceful 'k' and 'b' sounds used to describe his "cracked hands" that "ached / from labor" show that the father most likely had a tough, manual job. Because the father did "labor in the weekday weather" and then lit the fires on "Sundays too", it suggests that he never stopped working.

3) The poet uses a caesura to create a pause before this short sentence. This creates a feeling of honesty that emphasises the narrator's matter-of-fact tone.

4) The phrase suggests that the narrator did not express any of the gratitude or appreciation that they felt they should have. It

presents the narrator as being apathetic towards the father, as though they communicated but didn't engage with him.

5) The final stanza suggests that familial love can go unappreciated. This is shown through the word "lonely", which implies that the father's dutiful love for his family went unacknowledged and unreciprocated. The final stanza hints that the narrator may now understand that the love the father had for his family was shown through his sacrifices.

6) The final two lines reveal the narrator's sadness and guilt at not understanding the parental love the father displayed, as shown through the rhetorical question that makes up these lines. These emotions are emphasised through the repetition of the phrase "what did I know", as it suggests the narrator is almost choking on their words.

7) The poet uses a contrast between coldness and warmth to symbolise the emotional distance between the father and child. The "blueblack cold" reflects the emotional coldness and lack of communication between the narrator and their father. However, the father is presented as lighting the fires, reflecting his warmth and love, even though there is still little emotional love shown between him and his child.

8) The sonnet form usually consists of 14 lines, has a strict rhyme scheme and rhythm, and is traditionally used to express love for someone. However, the poet breaks the traditional conventions by having no rhyme scheme, an irregular metre, and not directly expressing love. This creates the sense that although the narrator now appreciates and has love for their father, this love was not expressed at the time.

Focus on... Sound

1) a) The phrase "banked fires blaze" is an example of alliteration.

b) The repetition of the forceful, plosive 'b' sound mimics the crackling of the wood as it burns, allowing the reader to share in the feeling of warmth the fires bring.

2) a) The word "splintering" is an example of onomatopoeia.

b) This imitates the sound of the fire burning and warming the air, which makes the memory seem more vivid.

3) The poet uses alliteration of the repeated 'w' sounds in "When the rooms were warm" and the long 'oh' sound in "slowly" to slow down the pace of the poem. This reflects the narrator lazily and slowly getting out of bed, which contrasts with the father who has already been up and active.

Exam-style Question — Part 2

You'll need to spend about 15 minutes on this, and your answer will probably bring in some of the things you thought about when you answered the other questions on the two poems. These are some points you could mention:

- In 'My Father on His Shield', the narrator's relationship with their father is presented as being emotionally strong although physically distant because of the father's death. This contrasts with 'Those Winter Sundays', in which the narrator is presented as being physically near to their father but lacking in emotional closeness.

- The narrator of 'My Father on His Shield' is presented as having an affectionate bond with their father. This is shown in the phrase "downhill we dived, // his boots by my boots", which uses the first-person plural pronoun "we" and the gentle internal rhyme of "by" and "my" to suggest emotional closeness between the narrator and father. In contrast, in 'Those Winter Sundays', the narrator's relationship with their father is characterised by the narrator's lack of appreciation. The phrase "No one ever thanked him" uses simple language to emphasise this harsh reality.

- The relationship in 'My Father on His Shield' is shown to be loving through literal closeness rather than communication. Although the father doesn't speak, he protectively wraps the "rope in his fist / around" the narrator's "chest". In contrast, the relationship in 'Those Winter Sundays' is shown to be less emotionally close as the narrator speaks "indifferently to" their father, as though they only speak to him because they must. The preposition "to" further suggests emotional distance between them, as it implies

Answers

a one-sided relationship where the father isn't listened to in return.

- The way each narrator presents their father doing strenuous activity shows their different attitudes. The narrator of 'My Father on His Shield' remembers their father's "fists, the iron he pounded, / five-pound hammer ringing steel", which uses forceful consonance and the onomatopoeic word "ringing" to indicate that the narrator is in awe of their father's strength and skill. In 'Those Winter Sundays', the narrator describes their father's "cracked hands that ached from labor". This uses consonance of the 'k' sound to mimic the splitting of the father's skin and emphasise the laborious nature of the father's work.

Section Three — Marking Sample Answers

Page 37 — Listen Mr Oxford Don

1) a) 6-7
   b) Two from, e.g.:
      • It explores the poet's use of language well.
      • It uses a range of relevant examples from the poem.
      • It uses technical terms accurately.
      • The point about the rhyming couplet could be developed further.

2) a) 8-9
   b) Two from, e.g.:
      • It makes critical comments on the poet's use of violent imagery.
      • It analyses several language features in detail.
      • It uses technical terms effectively.

3) a) 4-5
   b) Two from, e.g.:
      • It gives a clear answer to the question.
      • It uses plenty of quotes to support the argument.
      • The quotes aren't explored or analysed in detail.
      • It doesn't use many technical terms.

Page 39 — Neighbours

1) a) 8-9
   b) Two from, e.g.:
      • It convincingly compares the way the poets use structure to challenge prejudice.
      • It is well supported with examples from both poems.
      • It uses a variety of technical terms accurately.

2) a) 6-7
   b) Two from, e.g.:
      • It makes a thoughtful comparison of the poets' use of imagery.
      • It uses technical terms correctly.
      • It needs some more analysis of specific language features.

3) a) 4-5
   b) Two from, e.g.:
      • It makes a valid comparison between the two poems.
      • It uses relevant examples from both poems and gives some explanation of them.
      • The examples could be explored and analysed in more detail.
      • It could be improved with more technical terms.

Page 41 — Overlooking the River Stour

1) a) 8-9
   b) Two from, e.g.:
      • It gives an insightful analysis of the poem's form and structure.
      • It uses well-chosen examples to support its analysis.
      • It explores the way these techniques affect the reader.

2) a) 4-5
   b) Two from, e.g.:
      • It analyses the way in which the poet shows the narrator's distance from nature.
      • It uses relevant quotes.
      • It needs to use more technical terms.
      • It should comment more on the effect on the reader.

3) a) 6-7
   b) Two from, e.g.:
      • It explores the poet's techniques and examines the effects they create.

• It offers a thoughtful interpretation of the poem.
• The point about the combined words could be developed further.

Page 43 — Sonnet

1) a) 4-5
   b) Two from, e.g.:
      • It makes a comparison between the way the colours are used in the poems.
      • It uses relevant quotes to support the comparison.
      • It needs to use more technical terms.
      • The simile point could be developed in more detail.

2) a) 6-7
   b) Two from, e.g.:
      • It gives thoughtful analysis on the link between nature and relationships.
      • It gives some relevant examples and integrates them well.
      • It could use more close language analysis.
      • It could be improved with more technical terms.

3) a) 8-9
   b) Two from, e.g.:
      • It makes convincing comments on the way both poets use form.
      • It uses a wide range of relevant technical terms.
      • It makes reference to how the poetic techniques affect the reader.

Page 45 — Beat! Beat! Drums!

1) a) 4-5
   b) Two from, e.g.:
      • It gives a clear answer to the question.
      • It uses quotes to support the argument.
      • The quotes aren't explored or analysed in enough detail.
      • It could use more technical terms.

2) a) 8-9
   b) Two from, e.g.:
      • It explores the poet's use of contrasting language convincingly.
      • It explores the techniques the poet has used and their effect on the reader in detail.

Answers

- It uses a range of well-chosen examples to support its points.
- It uses technical terms effectively and convincingly.

3) a) 6-7
   b) Two from, e.g.:
   - It correctly identifies the form and structure of the poem and thoughtfully explains their significance.
   - It explains the techniques the poet has used.
   - It does not use enough quotes to support the points.
   - It could be improved with more technical terms.

Page 47 — Songs for the People

1) a) 6-7
   b) Two from, e.g.:
   - It makes good comparisons between the two poems.
   - It has a clear understanding of some of the poems' themes.
   - It uses some appropriate technical terms.
   - Some of the quotes are not integrated into the argument.

2) a) 8-9
   b) Two from, e.g.:
   - It convincingly compares the way the two poets use violent language.
   - It shows a clear understanding of the techniques used and the effect they have on the reader.
   - It uses technical terms correctly and effectively.

3) a) 4-5
   b) Two from, e.g.:
   - It compares the use of repetition in both poems.
   - It uses quotes from both poems to support its points.
   - None of the points are very well explained or developed. It would be better to focus on one point in detail, rather than covering lots very briefly.

Section Four — Practice Exam Questions

Page 48 — Time does not bring relief

1)
- In the poem, the narrator is stricken with grief at the loss of their male companion.
- When remembering their loved one, the narrator refutes the proverb that 'time heals all wounds' by stating in the opening line that "Time does not bring relief". This opening sets a negative tone for the rest of the poem and suggests that the sorrow caused by remembering a loved one will never ease.
- Punctuation is used to convey the narrator's grief. This can be seen through the use of end-stopping and caesura throughout the poem, which break the rhythm to hint at the narrator pausing, as if they have been overcome with emotion and have to stop to compose themselves. The pauses also force the reader to pause, inviting them to share in the narrator's grief.
- The poet's use of pathetic fallacy emphasises the narrator's grief. Human emotions are assigned to the weather in the metaphor "I miss him in the weeping of the rain". Associating the rain with weeping evokes the image of a downpour of tears. This highlights the narrator's own grief and creates a feeling of empathy in the reader.
- The narrator is presented as not wanting to be reminded of their loved one. They describe how there are a "hundred places" that they "fear / To go" because the places "brim" with his memory. The word "brim" creates the sense that these memories are almost overwhelming for the narrator, and creates the image of the narrator's eyes 'brimming' with tears. Furthermore, by choosing to go to places where their loved one's face never "shone", the narrator actually ends up thinking about him in his absence.
- Repetition is used to show how often the narrator remembers their loved one. The repetition of "him" in "I miss him" and "I want him" in lines 3 and 4 emphasises how the narrator's life is strongly concerned with the memory of him. Further, the repetition of "every" in "every mountain-side" and "every lane" emphasises how all-consuming their grief for him is.
- Sound devices highlight the narrator's sadness when remembering a loved

one. For example, the repeated 'h' sound in the alliterative "Heaped on my heart" echoes the sound of the narrator sighing, which emphasises their feeling of despair.
- The poem is written in the Petrarchan sonnet form. This form typically offers a problem in the first 8 lines and a solution in the final 6, but Millay subverts this form by not presenting a solution and by having the narrator still "stand stricken" to emphasise their despair. Moreover, sonnets are typically associated with love, and so this use of form highlights the narrator's love and how it is ongoing in their grief.

Page 49 — Farewell, Sweet Dust

2)
- The narrator of 'Time does not bring relief' mourns the loss of their loved one, whereas the narrator of 'Farewell, Sweet Dust' is generally less sorrowful.
- In each poem, the narrator shows a sense of bereavement. In the final line of Millay's poem, the narrator says "And so stand stricken". The use of sibilance in this phrase places emphasis on the word "stricken", a word which uses the harsh 'k' sound to emphasise the pain of the narrator's grief. In Wylie's poem, however, the narrator states "Now I have lost you", which uses simple, monosyllabic language to hint at the narrator's sadness.
- The narrator of Millay's poem doesn't seem able to let their loved one go, whereas the narrator of Wylie's poem is more accepting. In Millay's poem, the repetition of "last year's" in lines 6 and 7 shows that the narrator longs to return to the past. However, in Wylie's poem, the narrator says it is "only fair to the rest of the earth" that their loved one's ashes are scattered. This suggests that they take comfort in the idea that they will return to the earth, something emphasised through the gentle imagery, such as the "plumed" clouds and "silver" rain.
- Both poets use wintry imagery to present the narrator's attitude. In Millay's poem, the narrator states how although "the old snows melt from every mountain-side", their "bitter loving must remain". This image of the melting snow shows

63

Answers

that while winter is turning into spring and life is moving on, the narrator can't move on in the same way. In Wylie's poem, however, the narrator describes how the "Snowflakes" will become "softer feathered" by their loved one's ashes, showing they take comfort in how the loss of their loved one will make the winter less harsh.

- In both poems, the use of second-person address reflects the extent to which each narrator has or hasn't come to terms with their loss. In the first two lines of Millay's poem, the narrator says "you all have lied", which creates an accusatory tone and heightens the pain they feel. In contrast, the narrator of Wylie's poem talks to their loved one, such as in the phrase "I made you mine". This interaction with their loved one create a gentle, soothing mood, suggesting the narrator is more accepting of their loss. The second-person address helps the reader to understand both narrators' emotions even though they have different attitudes.

Page 50 — Solitude

1)

- In the poem, isolation is presented as a negative experience which can arise because of sad feelings. One of the main themes in the poem is how grief and sadness have to be faced alone.

- Personification is used to highlight isolation. For example, the phrase "Laugh, and the world laughs with you" can be seen to personify the entire world to show how included someone can feel when they're happy. However, this personification also adds emphasis to the following line that when people "weep", they do so "alone". By creating such an exaggerated contrast, this personification heightens the sense of isolation that the poet conveys.

- The narrator suggests that isolation is heightened by the way society shuns those who feel negative emotions, as shown when you "Grieve" and people "turn and go". The phrase "turn and go" suggests that those grieving have been abandoned, characterising society as cold and unsympathetic. From this, the reader gets the sense that the poet

is encouraging others to try to think differently about their own actions when people are grieving.

- The poet presents isolation as a painful experience. This is shown by how we all will go through "the narrow aisles of pain." The metaphor of pain's "narrow aisles" creates a sense of claustrophobia that contrasts with the spacious comfort evoked by the "halls of pleasure" earlier in the poem. This contrast emphasises the uncomfortable nature of isolation, and by ending the poem with the word "pain", the poet leaves this as the reader's final impression of solitude and isolation.

- The use of sound emphasises the feeling of isolation. In the phrase "one by one we must all file on", the similarly sounding words "on" and "one" appear on the beat of the line. This rhythm echoes the sound of monotonous marching to create a dull, bleak tone that reflects the feelings people experience when they are isolated.

- Isolation is presented as universal. Although a general sense of isolation is created in the phrase "one by one", the use of the first-person plural "we" in "we must all file on" reminds the reader that everybody experiences the same sense of isolation, inviting them to take comfort in knowing that they are not the only one who is alone.

- Juxtaposition emphasises the narrator's message about isolation. This can be seen through the pairs of imperatives that run throughout the poem, such as "Laugh" and "Weep", and "Sing" and "Sigh". These pairs appear at the start of lines and so are visually close together. By juxtaposing the effects of isolation with more joyous verbs in this way, the poet emphasises the anguish caused by isolation and suggests to the reader how quickly fulfilment can turn into isolation.

Page 51 — Ode on Solitude

2)

- The narrators of the two poems present contrasting views towards being alone. While the narrator of 'Solitude' presents it as unpleasant, the narrator of 'Ode on Solitude' shows that it can be fulfilling.

- The narrator of Wilcox's poem presents being alone as an unhappy experience. This is shown in the phrase "Sigh, it is lost on the air", as the onomatopoeic verb "Sigh" hints at the sadness people feel when they are alone. In contrast, the narrator of Pope's poem suggests people should embrace being alone. They state "Happy the man" who lives on their "own ground", which shows how being alone and self-sufficient can be satisfying.

- The poems' rhyme schemes reflect each presentation of being alone. In 'Solitude', the ABCBDEFE rhyme scheme has four unrhymed lines per stanza, which reminds the reader of the uncomfortable feeling people can experience when alone. In contrast, the ABAB rhyme scheme in 'Ode on Solitude' reflects the poem's sense of fulfilment. Every line has another that rhymes with it, reflecting the sense of comfort the narrator feels when they are alone.

- The use of repetition reflects each poem's message about being alone. In Wilcox's poem, the repetition in "Weep, and you weep alone" emphasises the despair people experience when they feel alone, as the alliteration of 'w' mimics the sound of crying. However, in Pope's poem, the anaphora of "Whose" in the second stanza emphasises how living a self-sufficient lifestyle can be enjoyable, as it suggests a proud sense of ownership over everything in a person's life.

- Both poets use voice to convey their message. The use of the second-person pronoun "you" in 'Solitude' makes the reader feel singled out, which creates a similar feeling of uncomfortable isolation. However, the use of the plural pronoun "we" later in the poem suggests that feeling alone is universal, and gives the reader the sense that the narrator feels alone too. In Pope's poem, the third-person singular "his" in the first stanza singles out the unnamed figure to describe the ideal life solitude can bring. However, the switch to the first person in the final stanza ("let me live, unseen") creates the sense that the narrator is also wishing for a similar lifestyle of solitude.

Answers

Glossary

alliteration	Where words that are close together start with the same sound, e.g. "perfumed papers".
ambiguity	Where a word or phrase has two or more possible interpretations.
anaphora	Where a word or phrase is repeated at the start of sentences or lines.
assonance	When words share the same vowel sound but their consonants are different, e.g. "anxiety stirred like a loose tooth".
blank verse	Poetry that is written in iambic pentameter and doesn't rhyme.
caesura (plural caesurae)	A pause in a line of poetry. E.g. the full stop in "It couldn't lie. Fell thick".
colloquial language	Informal language that sounds like ordinary speech, e.g. *"too bloody deep for me"*.
consonance	Repetition of a consonant sound in nearby words, e.g. "cracked hands that ached".
cyclical structure	Where key elements at the start of the text repeat themselves at the end.
dialect	A variation of a language spoken by people from a particular place or background. Dialects might include different words or sentence constructions, e.g. "So mek dem send".
direct address	When the narrator speaks directly to the reader or another character, e.g. "listen Mr Oxford don"
direct speech	The actual words that are said by someone.
emotive	Something that makes you feel a particular emotion.
end-stopping	Finishing a line of poetry with the end of a phrase or sentence, usually marked by punctuation.
enjambment	When a sentence or phrase runs over from one line or stanza to the next.
first person	Writing from the perspective of the narrator, written using words like 'I', 'me', 'we' and 'our'.
form	The type of poem, e.g. a sonnet or ballad, and its features, like number of lines, rhyme and rhythm.
free verse	Poetry that doesn't rhyme and has no regular rhythm or line length.
half-rhymes	Words that have a similar, but not identical, end sound. E.g. "bread" and "shade".
hyperbole	The use of exaggeration to emphasise a point.
iambic pentameter	Poetry with a metre of ten syllables — five of them stressed, and five unstressed. The stress falls on every second syllable, e.g. "For though from out our bourne of Time and Place".
iambic tetrameter	Like iambic pentameter but with a metre of eight syllables — four stressed and four unstressed. E.g. "We slowly drove – He knew no haste".
imagery	Language that creates a picture in your mind. It includes metaphors, similes and personification.
internal rhyme	When two or more words rhyme, and at least one of the words isn't at the end of a line. The rhyming words can be in the same line or nearby lines. E.g. "On all at stake, can undertake".
irony	When words are used to imply the opposite of what they normally mean. It can also mean when there is a difference between what people expect and what actually happens.
juxtaposition	When a poet puts two ideas, events, characters or descriptions close to each other to encourage the reader to contrast them. E.g. the juxtaposition of "Sing" and "Sigh" in 'Solitude'.
metaphor	A way of describing something by saying that it is something else, e.g. "narrow aisles of pain". An extended metaphor is a metaphor that is carried on, e.g. the tattoos metaphor in 'Tattoos'.
metre	The arrangement of stressed and unstressed syllables to create rhythm in a line of poetry.
monosyllables	Words with only one syllable, e.g. "Now I have lost you".

Glossary

Glossary

mood	The feel or atmosphere of a poem, e.g. humorous, peaceful, fearful.
narrative	Writing that tells a story, e.g. 'Because I could not stop for Death'.
narrative viewpoint	The perspective that a text is written from, e.g. first-person point of view.
narrator	The person speaking the words. E.g. the narrator of 'Listen Mr Oxford Don' is an immigrant.
onomatopoeia	A word that sounds like the thing it's describing, e.g. "whirr" and "thump".
oxymoron	A phrase which appears to contradict itself, e.g. "fierce lovely water".
pathetic fallacy	Giving human emotions to objects or aspects of nature, in order to create a certain mood. E.g. in 'Time does not bring relief', the "weeping of the rain" creates a mournful atmosphere.
personification	Describing a non-living thing as if it's a person. E.g. "this rain had forgotten the sea".
Petrarchan sonnet	A form of sonnet in which the first eight lines have a regular ABBA rhyme scheme and introduce a problem, while the final six lines have a different rhyme scheme and solve the problem.
phonetic spellings	When words are spelt as they sound rather than with their usual spelling, e.g. "dem" instead of "them". It's often used to show that someone is speaking with a certain accent or dialect.
plosive	A short burst of sound made when you say a word containing the letters b, d, g, k, p or t.
rhetorical question	A question that doesn't need an answer, but is asked to make or emphasise a point. E.g. "What did I know, what did I know / of love's austere and lonely offices?"
rhyme scheme	A pattern of rhyming words in a poem. E.g. 'Crossing the Bar' has an ABAB rhyme scheme — this means that the first and third lines in each stanza rhyme, and so do the second and fourth lines.
rhyming couplet	A pair of rhyming lines that are next to each other, e.g. lines 4 and 5 of 'Listen Mr Oxford Don'.
rhythm	A pattern of sounds created by the arrangement of stressed and unstressed syllables.
second person	When the narrator talks directly to another person, written using words like "you".
sensory language	Language that appeals to any of the five senses. "I let a different cleverness wash my tongue."
sibilance	Repetition of 's' and 'sh' sounds, e.g. "the sun surfacing".
simile	A way of describing something by comparing it to something else, usually by using the words "like" or "as". E.g. "steam billowing like a smoke screen".
sonnet	A form of poem with fourteen lines, that usually follows a clear rhyme scheme.
stanza	A group of lines in a poem.
structure	The order and arrangement of ideas and events in a poem, e.g. how it begins, develops and ends.
syllable	A single unit of sound within a word. E.g. "all" has one syllable, "always" has two.
symbolism	When an object stands for something else. E.g. the sunset in 'Crossing the Bar' symbolises the end of the narrator's life, and the drums in 'Beat! Beat! Drums!' symbolise war.
syntax	The arrangement of words in a sentence or phrase so that they make sense.
theme	An idea or topic that's important in a poem. E.g. a poem could be based on the theme of love.
third person	When a poet writes about someone who isn't the speaker, written using words like "he" or "she".
tone	The mood or feelings suggested by the way the narrator writes, e.g. bitter, reflective.
voice	The characteristics of the person narrating the poem. Poems are usually written either using the poet's voice, as if they're speaking to you directly, or the voice of a character.
volta	A turning point in a poem, when the argument or tone changes dramatically.

Acknowledgements

We would like to thank the following copyright holders:

Cover quote from 'Beat! Beat! Drums!' by Walt Whitman

'The Road Not Taken' by Robert Frost from Poetry of Robert Frost by Robert Frost. Published by Jonathan Cape. Reprinted by permission of The Random House Group Limited.
Digital permission of 'The Road Not Taken' by Robert Frost from THE POETRY OF ROBERT FROST edited by Edwards Connery Lathem. Copyright © 1916, 1969 by Henry Holt and Company. Copyright © 1944 by Robert Frost. Reprinted by permission of Henry Holt and Company. All Rights Reserved.

'Tattoos' from Selected Poems by Brian Patten. Published by Penguin, 2007. Copyright © Brian Patten.
Reproduced by permission of the author c/o Rogers, Coleridge & White Ltd., 20 Powis Mews, London W11 1JN

'The Ageing Schoolmaster' by Vernon Scannell. Reproduced by kind permission of the Vernon Scannell Literary Estate.

'Originally' from The Other Country by Carol Ann Duffy. Published by Anvil Press Poetry, 1990. Copyright © Carol Ann Duffy. Reproduced by permission of the author c/o Rogers, Coleridge & White Ltd., 20 Powis Mews, London W11 1JN

'Hard Water' by Jean Sprackland. Published by Jonathan Cape. © 2003 The Random House Group Limited.

'Island Man' by Grace Nichols from The Fat Black Woman's Poems. Copyright © Grace Nichols 1984 (Curtis Brown Ltd, London).

'Remember' by Joy Harjo. Copyright © 1983 by Joy Harjo, from SHE HAD SOME HORSES by Joy Harjo.
Used by permission of W.W. Norton & Company, Inc.

Walt MacDonald's poem, 'My Father on His Shield' is from the collection, Blessings the Body Gave (1998), and is reprinted with permission from the Ohio State University Press.

'Those Winter Sundays'. Copyright © 1966 by Robert Hayden, from COLLECTED POEMS OF ROBERT HAYDEN by Robert Hayden, edited by Frederick Glaysher. Used by permission of Liveright Publishing Corporation.

'Listen Mr Oxford Don' by John Agard from Propa Propaganda (Bloodaxe Books, 1996)
Reproduced with permission of Bloodaxe Books. www.bloodaxebooks.com

'Neighbours' by Benjamin Zephaniah from Alternative Anthem: Selected Poems with Live DVD (Bloodaxe Books, 2009)
Reproduced with permission of Bloodaxe Books. www.bloodaxebooks.com

THE POEMS OF EMILY DICKINSON: READING EDITION, edited by Ralph W. Franklin, Cambridge, Mass.: The Belknap Press of Harvard University Press, Copyright © 1998, 1999 by the President and Fellows of Harvard College. Copyright © 1951, 1955 by the President and Fellows of Harvard College. Copyright © 1979, 1983 by the President and Fellows of Harvard College. Copyright © 1914, 1918, 1924, 1929, 1930, 1932, 1935, 1937, 1942 by Martha Dickinson Bianchi. Copyright © 1952, 1957, 1958, 1963, 1965 by Mary L. Hampson.

Every effort has been made to locate copyright holders and obtain permission to reproduce sources.
For those sources where it has been difficult to trace the copyright holder of the work, we would be grateful
for information. If any copyright holder would like us to make an amendment to the acknowledgements,
please notify us and we will gladly update the book at the next reprint. Thank you.